M000159719

The Servant King
A Study of the Gospel of Luke

By Hope A. Blanton and Christine B. Gordon

19Baskets

The Servant King
A Study of the Gospel of Luke
© 2022 by Hope A. Blanton and Christine B. Gordon
ISBN 978-1-946862-17-4

19Baskets, Inc.
PO Box 31291
Omaha, NE 68131
https://19baskets.com

First Edition

Cover design by Sophie Calhoun

Photography by Jen Hinrichs

Unless otherwise indicated, all Scripture quotations are from the Holy Bible, English Standard Version® (ESV®), copyright © 2001 by Crossway. Used by permission. All rights reserved.

Contents

At His Feet Story

A few years ago, Hope started looking for materials for the women's fall Bible study at our church. While she found a great number of quality Bible studies, she had a hard time finding studies written for women by women who were reformed. She also had a tough time finding in-depth studies of the Scripture that didn't take a whole lot of time. In a moment of desperation, Hope asked Chris if she would be willing to co-write a study on Romans, convincing her by asking, "I mean, really, how hard could it be?" And so it began. Weekly emails back and forth, Chris deep in commentaries, Hope mulling over questions, tweaking, editing, asking, pondering. A group of women at Redeemer Presbyterian Church in Lincoln, Nebraska, patiently bore with us as we experimented with them every week and learned to find our rhythm as writers.

Two years later, Hope approached Chris again, softening her up by telling her she could choose any book she wanted: 1 Samuel it was. Old Testament narrative is the best. Another study was born. About this time, women started asking us for copies of the two studies we had written. While we were trying to send endless pdfs to people around the country via email, a pastor friend who happens to be a publisher approached us at a party, offering to publish the Bible studies. Suddenly, we had a way to get these into the hands of women who could use them. This had been the point of the whole enterprise—to help make the Bible more accessible to women. But what would the name be?

During the first century, when Jesus walked the earth, a Jewish rabbi would have been surrounded by his students, with some of the men sitting as his feet to learn and listen. This was the custom, the understood norm of the day. But in Luke 10:39, *Mary* sat at the feet of Jesus. Mary, a woman, was taught by this

1

unconventional rabbi. Mary was given the dignity of taking in his words, his pauses, his tone. To Jesus, she was every bit as worthy of his teaching as the men in the room were—and so are we, his women students today. And so we are At His Feet Bible Studies, hoping to sit at the feet of Jesus while we study his Word.

Please find our other available studies at our website:
www.athisfeetonline.com

User Guide

There is no right way to lead a Bible study. Every Bible study group is made up of different types of women with various sets of needs and dynamics. Below are some suggestions that might be helpful when using At His Feet Studies. Read it through. Use what you want. Forget the rest. We're glad you're here.

Participants Guide

This study is laid out like most commentaries. Each chapter is broken up into smaller portions with explanations of the verses in order. There are questions in the chapters before and after the commentary. The first set of questions are Observation Questions designed to help you interact with the basic content of the chapter. The second set of questions are Reflection Questions designed to help you engage your heart with the text in a vulnerable way.

Start by reading the Scripture passage noted at the top of the study page. Then answer the Observation Questions. Next, go back and read the Scripture side by side with the commentary, pausing between each grouping of verses to absorb both the commentary and the text more deeply. Then move on to answer the Reflection Questions.

Leaders Guide

There are nine questions for each study. When in a group setting, we suggest choosing your favorite Reflection Questions to focus on, especially if you run short on time. If you have more time feel free to work through all the questions. For those groups where people have not had the time and space to read through the

3

commentary and questions, you can simply read the commentary out loud at the beginning of your time. That way all women can participate. We always suggest reading the Scripture passage out loud before you begin.

Extras

The focus verse is something to spend time reflecting on since it's the heart of the passage. Consider memorizing it individually or as a group.

Use the section we have labeled "Reflections, curiosities, frustrations" to write down things about the text that seem confusing to you or hard for you to wrap your brain around. This is meant to give you space to express how you're a work in progress as you work through this text and engage with God's Word.

Introduction

At some point in our lives, most of us have read or listened to some or all of the Gospel of Luke. Maybe you recited the birth announcement to the shepherds in a Christmas pageant as a child. Maybe you've seen verses painted on crafty banners for sale. Maybe you've studied the entire Book of Luke. It can be tempting to gloss over familiar passages like many we find in Luke's gospel. We've heard them before. We could recite parts of them. We already know the story.

But how well do you know the one in the story? When was the last time you came face to face with the Jesus of the Gospels and were in awe? When was the last time his actions took your breath away? Have his words shocked you lately? Have his commands prompted your repentance? Have his promises made your heart long with hope? It is our hearts that grow dull, not his story. He is just as vibrant and alive as our souls ache for him to be. As you meet him afresh in his Word, pray that his Spirit would attend your reading and give you ears to hear. You will find him wildly captivating, unceasingly lovely.

Before diving into the text, a few observations and comments will help us prepare.

Who was Luke anyway? It may seem strange at first to read a book by someone who isn't even mentioned in the Bible until Paul speaks of him in Colossians 4:14 as "the beloved physician." But Luke was no stranger to the story of Jesus's life. He was a traveling companion of Paul and was imprisoned with him for two years in Caesarea. Both the "we" sections of Acts and hundreds of years of tradition confirm for us that Luke and Paul spent much time together.

But Luke was not the typical biblical author. For starters, he may have been a Gentile. He never met Jesus but was converted by the early church. Luke lived in the first century AD and probably wrote his Gospel between 60 and 70 AD. He was clearly an educated man, as his gospel's prologue (Luke 1:1-4) was written in classical Greek, probably the most formal Greek in the New Testament. In Luke 1:5, he switches to koine Greek, the common Greek language of his day.

How is Luke's gospel different from those of Matthew, Mark, and John? First, Luke's is the longest of the Gospels, and it is the only one with a sequel—the Book of Acts. Luke and Acts together make up more than one-quarter of the entire New Testament. Clearly God gave this man a large amount of influence. Second, Luke sets his telling of the story of redemption firmly in the context of world history. He cites particular names and titles of rulers, geographical markers, and dates to embed the life and ministry of Jesus in wider history. For example, in Luke 3:1-2, Luke cites six historical markers for the reader before he begins his narrative about John the Baptist. Luke is a careful historian, stating his desire to put together "an orderly account." He uses primary source material, including testimony of eyewitnesses. Some commentators think it is entirely possible that he interviewed Mary for the birth narrative.

Third, Luke's gospel is for everyone: Gentiles, women, the poor, the disreputable. Concerning the Gentiles: While Matthew writes his genealogy beginning with Abraham, the father of the Jews (Matthew 1), Luke writes his genealogy ending with Adam, the father of all humans (Luke 3). Concerning women: In the first eight chapters alone, Luke tells the birth story of Jesus from Mary's perspective, explains her encounter with Elizabeth, mentions Anna the prophetess, and tells the stories of raising the widow's son, the woman who anoints Jesus's feet, the woman who is healed of her bleeding, and the women who travel with Jesus. All of this in an age when most women were considered secondary and all Jewish men began their day with this prayer to God: "Thank you that you have not made me a Gentile, a slave, or a woman." Concerning the poor and disreputable: Luke points out the "unclean" people of society and Jesus's ministry to them multiple times. He explains that Jesus's birth announcement was to unclean shepherds. He highlights the way Jesus touches and heals lepers and the demon-possessed.

Luke is clearly painting a picture of salvation that is available for everyone, not just the Jews. This is the story of redemption in vivid colors and shocking contrast. This is the story of Jesus, who came to die, to rise, to reign. He came to love us, the servant king.

Reflection Questions

1. Have you ever read part or all of the Gospel of Luke? How would you describe the book?

2. Do you have a favorite passage from Luke? If so, which one?

3. Of all the information you read in the introduction, what did you learn that really stood out to you? Why?

4. What are you hoping studying Luke will do for your heart over the course of completing this Bible study?

Introduction

Reflections, curiosities, frustrations:

Study 1

The Lowly King

Read Luke 1–3

Observation Questions

1. List the details of what happened to Elizabeth, Zechariah, and Mary and how their stories are connected (Luke 1:5–80). What similar themes appear in both Zechariah's and Mary's songs of praise?

2. What happened the day Jesus was circumcised at the temple (who was there, what they each did, etc.)?

3. Describe the day when Jesus was twelve years old and stayed behind in Jerusalem (who was there, what they each did, etc.).

4. From Luke 3:21-22, write the specific details of Jesus's baptism.

Luke 1:1-25. For over four hundred years, no one heard from the God who had promised to send the Messiah, a savior to rescue his people. There were no visions, no prophets, no word from Yahweh. The ritual of offering sacrifices to God had continued. The temple still stood. The feasts of Israel, the Sabbaths, the telling of the stories of the Exodus went on. But it must have felt like God had forgotten his people. Enter Zechariah. Having been born in a line of priests, Zechariah would have gone to the temple in Jerusalem twice per year to perform whatever priestly duty was chosen by lot. This time he was chosen to burn the incense, which symbolized the prayers of Israel going up to God and was an immense honor that a priest would perform only once in his life. For Zechariah this would have been the high point of his existence. For just a few moments this man was to be as close to God as any human at the time could get. He and all of the worshippers waiting for him would have been praying for the salvation of Israel.

Zechariah and Elizabeth were way past child-bearing age, but still God had given them no children. Zechariah may have given up praying for a child, but his name means "the Lord has remembered."[1] And in the darkness of the holy place with incense filling his nostrils, Zechariah learned that God's remembering of Israel would include an individual remembrance of him. This is how our God works. He uses our stories, our losses, our longings, our voices, and our prayers to further his kingdom. When Zechariah voiced his doubt, the angel rebuked him. It is as if Zechariah was saying, "But I'm old," and the angel was saying, "But he's God." This is the first of countless glimpses of the upside-down kingdom in Luke. God's first words to the world after centuries involved an infertile couple having a baby who would prepare the way for the savior of the world.

Luke 1:26–56. The scene changes from inside Jerusalem's temple to the countryside and a little town called Nazareth. Unlike today, where the majority of people are engaged to be married in their twenties and thirties, betrothal usually happened soon after puberty. Mary was probably in her early teens. Notice in verse 28 how the angel greets Mary. "Favored one" here is not a status Mary had earned. Mary was not chosen because she did something right. God gave her this honor in the same way he gives all believers honor—not from any merit of their own.

Mary was voiceless as a girl in her culture, powerless to change her status in life. The God of the universe who made billions of stars and called them out by name chose to house himself in the fragile confines of a teenage girl's delicate womb. Oh, the

---

[1] Walter L. Liefeld and David W. Pao, "Luke," in *Luke-Acts*, vol. 10 of *The Expositor's Bible Commentary*, rev. ed., edited by Tremper Longman III and David E. Garland (Grand Rapids, MI: Zondervan, 2006), 54.

humility, the mind-boggling plans of the Lord. He will not act according to our expectations or be restricted by our imaginations. The silence had been broken. The servant king was coming. This teenager had to have been overwhelmed by her own news and curious about that of her elderly relative. Mary began a four-day journey to visit Elizabeth, giving her plenty of time to ponder the way God was weaving together her story. She had time, as she walked, to think about what the angel had said in terms of what she already knew about God. She would have known the stories of the Israelites, the story of Hannah, the hope of a Messiah to come.

When Elizabeth heard Mary's greeting and felt the baby in her womb leap for joy in response, Elizabeth understood the grand story of which she was a part. The upside-down kingdom had come to her little town. And the king of the upside-down kingdom, tucked in underneath the heart of a teenage girl, had just entered her house. Elizabeth's acknowledgment of the "Lord" was not lost on Mary. Her excitement and joy could no longer be contained. Mary burst out in a song that is remarkably similar to Hannah's song in 1 Samuel 1, which she would have known since childhood. This is the Magnificat, a Latin word that literally means "enlarge." Mary could not help but worship as she acknowledged the privilege she had been given as mother of the Messiah. She sings about the way God is turning the world upside down, bringing down the proud, giving the humble power, and filling the stomachs of the poor.

Luke 1:57-80. The day of a boy's circumcision was like our present-day infant baptism. Friends and relatives would have been invited to join the ceremony, which signified the fact that all of God's promises were now applicable to this individual child. It was also the day when the baby received his name from the parents. These parents both gave a name with no familial history. This was a break with tradition, a statement of God breaking in and calling

John to something different. Notice that Zechariah's first words after months of silence were words of praise. Filled with the Holy Spirit, he sang first about God keeping his promises to his people and then about his little son's calling to pave the way for the Messiah.

Most devout Jews believed that someone would come prior to the Messiah, an Elijah figure to prepare the way. Zechariah recognized John as this figure. God was answering both Zechariah's prayer for a child and his prayer for the deliverance of Israel. His song, like Mary's, spoke prophetically of things that were to come as if they had already happened. His song is one of overwhelming, relieved joy. See the power, sovereignty, tenderness, and attention of our God. He is always working—both in our individual stories and in the bigger story of deliverance for his people. Just when we think there is nothing to be done, he breaks through our expectations. What can our response be but that of Mary and Zechariah? We praise him. We marvel at the way our God orders history, even our own individual lives.

Luke 2:1–40. Luke lays out the kingdom of man and the kingdom of God side by side. Augustus changed the Roman republic into an empire and asserted himself as a "son of God" and "the savior of the world." The true Son of God was lying in a feeding trough. He was the child of a poor couple, and they had no one else to wrap the baby in the traditional cloths, a job usually done by a midwife. He may have been born in a cave, the bottom floor of a house, or an open courtyard. These two kingdoms could not have been more different. Augustus was building and displaying power for his own good. God was entering into the brokenness of the world for our good. Most royal births are announced with lavish ceremonies. This baby came with a holy army who sang to the outcasts. Shepherds were dirty, poor, and always ceremonially unclean because of their work. These shepherds, these unwanted people, were the recipients of the best news ever: The war between God and men was over; God was going to make peace—real peace.

Leviticus 12 tells us that when a woman had a baby, she was to bring a lamb as a burnt offering and a pigeon or turtle dove for a sin offering to make atonement for herself. However, if she could not afford a lamb, she could bring another pigeon or turtle dove instead. This, the offering Mary and Joseph brought, was called the "Offering of the Poor." The one who authored history, marked the boundaries of the sea, and owned the cattle on a thousand hills was born into a family that couldn't afford a lamb. And although his parents were a devout part of the remnant of Israel, they also probably struggled to put food on the table consistently. Jesus, from the very beginning of his humanity, dealt with the problem of suffering by entering into it.

Luke 2:41-52. Travel caravans of Jesus's day would have been made up of many families traveling together and would have been divided between the men, who walked faster, and the women and children, who traveled much more slowly. Since Jesus was just on the cusp of manhood, each parent could have easily assumed he was with the other group. Every adult male who lived within fifteen miles of Jerusalem was required by Jewish law to attend the Passover. At twelve, Jesus was considered a man. He would have understood the purpose of the blood and the ritual, the need for cleansing and forgiveness. Somehow, his self-awareness had grown to the point that when his parents returned to find him, Jesus's first words included referring to God as Father, instead of his earthly father, Joseph.

The temple was the regular place where teachers would have gathered to discuss the Scriptures. While Mary was rushed and panicked, Jesus was calm. His understanding of the Scriptures and God amazed the theological experts of his day. His parents, the people who knew him best, completely misunderstood him at this moment. Isn't this true for us? We have experiences that cause us to believe we know Jesus, that we've figured him out. And then he surprises us.

Luke 3:1-20. Eighteen years had passed since Jesus had called the living God his Father while sitting at the temple in Jerusalem. The word of God had come to John. Little is said about this last great prophet, but his message is clear: Get ready. Judgment is coming. You must repent. John was the courier, the hype man, the forerunner for Jesus. He quoted Isaiah 40:3-5, encouraging the people to ready themselves for the coming king. In ancient times, when kings wanted to visit a portion of their territory, they would send a courier ahead to those along the way instructing them to fill in the holes, straighten the road, build bridges, cut down trees, and prepare a path so that the king could get to them. But Jesus was a different kind of king, requiring a different kind of preparation.

John's harsh words were directed toward those Jews who thought that their spiritual pedigree was a free ticket into the kingdom. Baptism in John's day was a ceremony used for unclean Gentiles converting to Judaism. It would have been offensive to the Jews to hear John preach of their need for such a rite, since they believed they were already "in."

John did not instruct the people to quit their jobs or destroy the system in which they worked, but to do their jobs in a conscientious and ethical way. Those who had enough were to share with those who did not. Tax collectors who made a living by taking extra money were only to take what they needed. Real repentance isn't a feeling or mere words. It has teeth, action, and visible change. Teachers were often paid not with money in ancient Palestine but with favors. According to a rabbinic saying, anything a slave would do for his master was a fair expectation of a disciple for his teacher, except for one task: untying a sandal thong. Loosing dirty foot straps was too degrading even for a disciple. But the servant king that was coming would be like no teacher anyone had ever served. No task would be menial in his service.

Luke 3:21–38. Just as Jesus had chosen to join himself to sinners in his birth, so he chose to identify with sinners by being baptized. He is always coming nearer to us. In a moment of amazing intimacy displayed for all around, God affirmed his Son and his ministry. "You are my beloved Son" is a part of Psalm 2:7, a description of the Messiah. Even on this day, the public beginning of his ministry, Jesus knew where he was going—he was beginning the road to the cross.

It is easy for us to forget that while Jesus was fully God, he was also fully human. Though he clearly understood something of his identity in the temple at age twelve, Jesus returned with his parents to Nazareth, submitted to their authority, and waited. He knew long hours and lean meals. Hebrews 5:8 tells us, "Although he was a son, he learned obedience through what he suffered." The king himself entered into the tiresome, mundane tasks of everyday life. And although he was without sin, he suffered in all the ways we do, in the brokenness of the world he came to save.

The four-hundred-year silence of God had been broken with the promise of a baby to an old man serving in the temple. The Second Person of the Trinity housed himself in the body of a teenage girl, grew as a boy, submitted to his parents, and learned the Scriptures. He was baptized with sinners and lived in poverty with his family. The king of heaven had entered the pain of earth in order to redeem all things and all people. He came to die, to rise, to reign. He came to love us, the servant king.

Reflection Questions

5. Reflect on the thought that for over four hundred years there were no visions, no prophets, no word from Yahweh, only rituals and routines to maintain a connection to the Lord. How must those four hundred years have felt? How does it make you view the spiritual habits we use on a regular basis in a different light?

6. God answered both the individual prayer of Zechariah for a son and the collective prayers of Israel for a Messiah together in one story. What are some things that this shows us about the character of our God?

7. The unclean, untrustworthy, unwanted shepherds were the first to be greeted by a host of angels to tell them that the Messiah had come. What do you think God is trying to communicate about the gospel through this scene? Have you found this to be true of the gospel?

8. Jesus surprised his parents when he chose not to leave Jerusalem when they did, showing them that who they thought he was, and how he should act, looked different than expected. When has your idea of who you thought Jesus was shifted or changed? Why?

9. At Jesus's baptism we get to see this very tender, intimate proclamation of God toward his Son, connecting back to Scriptures the Jews would have known describing the Messiah. What does this moment show us about God the Father toward Jesus his Son? How does that connect to us?

Focus verse: *Blessed be the Lord God of Israel, for he has visited and redeemed his people and has raised up a horn of salvation for us in the house of his servant David.*
Luke 1:68–69

Reflections, curiosities, frustrations:

Study 2

The Healing King

Read Luke 4–6

Observation Questions

1. Luke 4:31-44 describes the beginning of Jesus's ministry. List some of the things he did.

2. Describe what happened when Jesus called the first of his twelve disciples (Luke 5:1–11).

3. In Luke 6:1–11, what are two things Jesus did on the Sabbath? Who disagreed with him for this? Why?

4. List the things Jesus said to do for others in Luke 6:27–36.

Luke 4:1-21. Jesus went from a climactic spiritual high to a wretched, arduous low. Notice that the Spirit led Jesus into the desert to be tempted. God always tests and readies his chosen leaders before using them. He did the same thing with his Son. In the midst of this wrestling, Satan, the master of deception, inserted himself, offering things that were attractive, alternatives that seemed to meet legitimate needs but that actually would have led away from dependency on and obedience to God. Followers of Jesus will live this same life of testing, wrestling, and being formed by the Spirit. All testing reveals our hearts. In these temptations, Jesus's heart was revealed to be pure, ready to accept the cross, and utterly dependent on his Father.

Jesus went on a preaching tour, and when he got back to his hometown synagogue, he was asked to read from the Scriptures and make comments afterward, as all adult men did. Everyone who was in the synagogue that day knew Jesus, probably from the time he was a boy. Yet they had heard the reports and expected him to launch a plan for bringing down the corrupt political system of the Romans. They believed that the Jews were God's chosen people and that Gentiles were simply, as rabbis wrote, "fuel for the fires of hell."

Jesus read from Isaiah 61. "The year of the Lord's favor" would have reminded them of the Year of Jubilee, which happened once every fifty years. In that year, according to Leviticus 25, all debts were forgiven and slaves set free. Jesus said this: "Today this Scripture has been fulfilled in your hearing." Jesus was claiming to be the object of Isaiah's prophecy. He would rescue the Jews and put everyone else in their place. Or so they thought.

Luke 4:22–30. Jesus could have given the people exactly what they wanted—rescue from political oppression and some sort of favored, exclusive salvation for Jews. But Jesus was building a kingdom not for the Jews only but for all who would come to him. He knew they wanted signs; he knew he would anger them. And yet he boldly called them out. He confronted their prideful belief that God loved only them. Using the Scriptures they would have known, he pointed out God's pursuit of Gentiles even in the time of their ancestors. And it enraged them. They understood some sort of grace for their own kind, but this was too much. Grace extended to the dirty, ceremonially unclean Gentiles pushed them over the edge.

Before we judge these people for their clueless closed-mindedness, we might examine ourselves. Do we do this? Do we consider certain categories of people outside the realm of Jesus's grace?

Luke 4:31–44. Two things happened in Galilee at the synagogue that reveal Jesus's astonishing authority over all things. First, his teaching. Rabbis at the time of Jesus did most of their teaching by quoting rabbis that had come before them, and some did this exclusively. Jesus quoted no one except Old Testament writers. He simply spoke the truth about God. The people who listened to him had never heard anything like this.

Second, this authority extended to Jesus's interactions with demons. While many exorcised demons in his day, Jesus did not use magical words or strange ceremonies. He simply told the demon to shut up and come out. As we learn later in the Gospels, all authority had already been given to this king. He needed only to speak to make things happen.

In the same way, Jesus spoke to sickness, and it left. On the Sabbath, no work could be done by the Jews, including the work of carrying the sick. But when the sun set, the sick and demon-possessed found Jesus. See his tenderness, how he touched each individual as he healed them. Consider the dignity he bestowed on each person who approached him in desperation. Jesus used his authority to demonstrate for the people what God's kingdom and God's rule looked like. The upside-down kingdom was on display among the sick and the demon-possessed as the servant king preached his way through the synagogues of Judea.

Luke 5:1–11. Simon had heard Jesus's teaching and had seen his power, but Jesus was much more sure about Simon than Simon was about Jesus. Simon must have listened as Jesus taught the people that morning. After speaking, Jesus narrowed his focus to Simon alone, saying, "Put out into the deep and let down your nets for a catch." Simon was no amateur fisherman, and though he believed nothing would come of trying again at this point, he had seen enough of Jesus to know that he should listen.

The catch that resulted was the biggest any of the professional fishermen in those boats had ever seen. Simon could no longer hold in a response: "Depart from me, for I am a sinful man, O Lord," he said. If we see ourselves clearly when we see the blinding majesty and power of Jesus, this will be our response. The holiness of God and the sinfulness of humans cannot coexist. And yet, Jesus, already knowing all of the terrible parts of Simon, pursued him in a particular and personal way, calling him as a disciple.

Luke 5:12-26. It would be fair to assume this leper had not been touched in years. People with leprosy would have been estranged from family, unable to earn a living, sometimes disfigured, and definitely isolated. Notice Jesus's answer and touch: "I will; be clean." But Jesus didn't stop there. His command for the man to show himself to the priest and offer sacrifices would have ensured that the priest would examine him, declare him clean, and restore him to community. Jesus's healing is not only physical but emotional, relational, psychological, and spiritual.

Luke 5:27-39. As a tax collector, Levi was probably the wealthiest of the disciples. Levi invites his new Lord to spend time with his friends, who also would have been tax collectors. Tax collectors were hated. But while the Pharisees avoided such people in order to remain ceremonially clean, Jesus pursued them in order to make these unclean sinners beautifully holy.

Again, the Pharisees missed the point in their question to Jesus about fasting. Though fasting was only prescribed once per year by the law, the Pharisees made it their practice to fast twice per week. They were living as if it were a time to mourn for Israel, as if the kingdom had not yet come. But the kingdom had come. Jesus compares his presence to a wedding, something to be celebrated, not a time of mourning.

Luke 6:1–11. The ceremonial law was a means to an end, a signpost of something greater, a shadow of what is to come, but the Pharisees had made it an end in itself instead, missing the point. As they continued to try to trap Jesus, he showed them that he had authority over the law. One Sabbath, Jesus's followers ate some grain while walking through the fields. The Pharisees tried to indict Jesus for preparing food on the Sabbath, which was forbidden. But Jesus reminded them of the story of David and his companions eating the bread of the presence in the tabernacle (1 Samuel 21:6). He valued human need over ritual.

On another Sabbath, Jesus healed a man with a shriveled hand. While the Pharisees allowed healing on the Sabbath when someone was in danger of dying, this man wasn't, and they saw it as an opportunity to set Jesus up. Jesus knew their hearts and asked them a question, leaving no middle ground but only the choice to do good or evil. All their additions, explanations, and expansions of the law had turned God's holy law of love into something so unrecognizable that it blinded them from the chief purpose of the law. God gave the Sabbath to provide life-giving rest to the weary (Exodus 20:10), but they had turned it into an oppressive weapon. Jesus did not come to shame, trap, or catch you doing wrong. He came to save and lead his people into the Sabbath rest that remains for the people of God (Hebrews 4:9).

Luke 6:12–16. Jesus must have known that the religious establishment would find a way to kill him. How would he get the message of the kingdom out to the world before he was silenced? Jesus prayed, this time all night. Just as Moses came down from the mountain after spending time with God and spoke to the twelve tribes of Israel, Jesus came back to his disciples and chose twelve men.

Who were these spiritual giants called to be the first of a church that must endure until the Second Coming? Jesus chose ordinary, unexpected men: fishermen, a tax collector, a zealot who had probably encouraged revolutionary opposition to Rome. Jesus chose one who would betray him. Who builds a leadership team like this? Only one whose kingdom was nothing like the world had ever seen.

Luke 6:17-26. Everywhere Jesus went, crowds followed. They couldn't get enough of him. As he spoke, taught, and healed, Jesus had begun to show the crowds and especially his disciples a new kind of kingdom, a new way of community.

Jesus describes the values of the kingdom: powerlessness, neediness, grief, and exclusion. And he contrasts them with the values of the world: power, comfort, success, and recognition. Jesus completely turns the values of the world upside down.

"Blessed" here means "deeply satisfied." The conditions of neediness and dependency on God are the things that we should prize in the kingdom of God. In fact, when you are weak, needy, grieving, or excluded, the power and delight you have in Jesus somehow grows stronger.

"Woe to you" would be better translated, "how terrible" or "how awful." It's not that power, comfort, success, and recognition are bad things or things to be avoided in and of themselves. It is only that we must be suspect of them because they can encourage self-reliance and the belief that we are not needy for Jesus.

Luke 6:27–36. The type of love Jesus describes here the Greeks would have called *agape*. It is in no way related to the merits of the object, and it is not based on common interests or possible payback. Its aim is the absolute good of the object. This is the kind of love Jesus tells us to lavish on our enemies.

Agape makes decisions based on the good of its object. It is not blind to the faults and undeserving nature of its object but is strong and purposeful. It is seeking the good of others, even when they don't deserve it, and even when they don't seek yours. It is sacrificial.

This is a hard command, an extremely high calling, a call to be like God. If this does not give us pause, we have overestimated ourselves. If we truly listen to this command, we will find ourselves begging God to change us to be more like him.

Jesus is telling us that his followers cannot be selective in their love. We don't love with agape to gain access to God, or even to be rewarded by him, though he says we will be. We do so because God does so. We do so because "while we were enemies we were reconciled to God by the death of his Son" (Romans 5:10).

Luke 6:37-38. These verses have perpetually been taken out of context and used to encourage the giving of money, but Jesus is actually talking about giving mercy. He tells us that instead of following in the footsteps of the Pharisees and condemning others based on a standard we ourselves cannot keep, we should deal with our own sin and give mercy to others. And he is saying that when you generously give mercy to people when they sin against you, God will generously give mercy to you when you sin against him. In fact, his mercy to you will overflow.

Luke 6:39–42. While Jesus instructed his disciples to give mercy and refrain from judgment, the Pharisees and teachers of the law were doing the opposite. In the region of Palestine, water was a precious commodity. People would dig for water and, finding none, would abandon the holes as unmarked pits. Blind people, who were many, easily fell into these pits, often causing catastrophic injury. Jesus warns those listening that the religious leaders of the day were spiritually blind and that if people followed them, they, too, would eventually be blind like their leaders, leading to their destruction.

Jesus, the king of heaven, passed the test with Satan in the wilderness. He healed the sick, cast out demons, and called common men to be his disciples. He turned the world upside down with his teaching, angering the religious authorities and delighting the poor and the outcast. He came to die, to rise, to reign. He came to love us, the servant king.

Reflection Questions

5. Jesus has complete power and authority over all things, even demons and sickness. What about that is comforting to you? What about that is scary or unsettling?

6. Simon, after watching Jesus teach, heal, and get him the biggest catch of his lifetime, responded with, "Depart from me, for I am a sinful man, O Lord." Why do you think he responded this way? Have you ever felt this way when you have encountered Jesus?

7. The Pharisees, or "separated ones," were looking for the Messiah. Their rules kept them from seeing it was Jesus. How are you currently like them?

8. Jesus fulfilled the law in the deepest way by showing mercy and healing on the Sabbath. Why do you think this made the Pharisees angry? Can you relate to their reaction?

9. Which of these moments in the upside-down kingdom does your heart most need to engage with right now: calling of the fisherman, healing the untouchable, forgiving the paralytic, or associating with the outcasts? Why?

Focus verse: *But love your enemies, and do good, and lend, expecting nothing in return, and your reward will be great, and you will be sons of the Most High, for he is kind to the ungrateful and the evil. Be merciful, even as your Father is merciful.*
Luke 6:35–36

Reflections, curiosities, frustrations:

Study 3

The Compassionate King

Read Luke 7-8

Observation Questions

1. List all the details of the healing of the centurion's servant in Luke 7:1-10.

2. In Luke 7:18-23, who did John the Baptist send to talk to Jesus? And what was Jesus's response?

3. List the different types of soil and what they each represent in the parable of the sower (Luke 8:4-15).

4. List the details of what happened when Jesus healed Jairus's daughter in Luke 8:49-56 (who was there, what they each did, what was said, etc.).

In Luke 6, Jesus had been explaining what life looks like in the upside-down kingdom. Now in chapter 7, he would show them what it looked like in day-to-day life.

Luke 7:1-10. News was constantly spreading about Jesus's miracles, so it is no surprise that the stories would have reached the household of the centurion. Having been immersed in the culture for some time, the centurion knew to approach Jesus by sending Jewish elders to request his help. Notice the elders' argument as to why Jesus should come: The centurion was worthy (verse 5). This is usually our heart's assumption, that we deserve for God to do things for us. The centurion knew the truth, that he deserved nothing from Jesus.

The centurion also would have known that coming to the house of a Gentile like himself would have made Jesus ritually unclean, so before Jesus even got to his house, the centurion sent him a message. As a man of authority, the centurion would have regularly moved men into action simply by the power of his word, and he had deduced that Jesus could do the same. Just as the centurion had authority over men, he understood that Jesus had authority over sickness and death. He did not stumble with unbelief. He knew Jesus was able, so he asked. Jesus marveled at his faith.

Luke 7:11–17. At this time and place in history, her son's death would have sentenced this widow to poverty, with no opportunity to make a living. Piled on top of her heartbreak was the knowledge that she would soon be begging for food and would probably be homeless.

When Jesus saw her, he had compassion on her. This woman was the poor for whom he had come to proclaim good news (Luke 4:18). He felt compassion, and he did something about it that was unthinkable: He touched the body. Touching a dead body would render a Jew unclean for seven days and would require elaborate cleansing rituals to restore him. But the situation got even stranger. Jesus spoke to the dead man. And just as with the centurion's servant, Jesus's word was enough to restore the man's life.

These two stories of loss and redemption tell us some things about Jesus. First, Jesus feels deep compassion. The word used for compassion here is the strongest in the Greek language. This one who knew the glory of humans in their true state of happiness and joy before the Fall certainly felt immense sorrow as he watched them labor to navigate the brokenness of this world.

Second, Jesus is a man of both words and action. He is not some detached deity who guards himself from the mess of our lives.

He knows the implications and heaviness of our losses, and he does something about them. This is Jesus's compassion, a compassion that heals, reunites loved ones, and reverses death. This is the compassion that would eventually lead him to give himself on a cross in order to do something about all of the pain and loss and grief, to halt the tragic procession to the grave for all who believe in him.

Luke 7:18-30. Recall that a short time after baptizing Jesus, John was put into prison by Herod. He had not been present for Jesus's teaching or miracles. He, like most of Israel, expected the Messiah to set in motion a series of events with armies marching, governments falling, and sure judgment. The reports he was hearing about Jesus included none of the above. John was confused and discouraged.

John's disciples got a front-row seat to Jesus healing diseases, plagues, blindness, and exorcising demons. Jesus let his actions explain his identity. He was not bringing the kingdom that was expected. Instead of brute force and coercion, his kingdom would be governed by mercy and love. This was a complete paradigm shift, even for those who had been looking for the Messiah.

As John's disciples left, Jesus asked the crowds, Did you go into the desert to see a man easily swayed like a reed shaking in the wind? Or someone dressed for comfort and an easy life? No. You went to see the dividing line between one era and the next. The promises have come true; the Messiah has come.

Luke 7:31-35. Children who spent their days in the open market would act out scenes and would try to entice others to participate, playing a joyful flute for a wedding enactment or a sad dirge to depict a funeral. When other children refused to play as directed, they complained, accusing them of not being willing to play one way or the other. Jesus's words about his generation were not flattering. No matter how God came to them, they only complained and refused to listen. Neither the self-denying John nor the indulgent Jesus pleased the Pharisees. But, according to verse 35, there would be those who would see God in any approach.

Luke 7:36–50. Probably a former prostitute, this woman was used to judgment, the condemning looks, the pointing, the whispers. The woman had come with the intention of anointing Jesus's feet with expensive perfume, probably equivalent to about one year's wages. She wanted to express her love and gratitude by giving Jesus the most valuable thing she had. The norm was to pour this type of oil on the head. Pouring it on Jesus's feet was a mark of humility.

Probably more of a frequent entertainer of celebrities than a spiritual seeker, Simon sat silently judging both Jesus and the woman. Simon had offered Jesus none of the common courtesies regularly extended to guests in first-century Palestine. His invitation had the appearance of respect but was actually insulting. Jesus, of course, knew this, so he told a story that cut straight through Simon's smug, arrogant attitude, a parable that identified both Simon and the woman as debtors. The woman knew how much she owed. And she knew she could not pay. Just as the debt was cancelled in the story, the woman's debt of sin had been cancelled by Jesus. Her response was complete and total adoration, overflowing gratitude and love. But Simon thought his good deeds could balance out his bad ones, that by keeping the law he could pay back his debt. He thought he was a "good person" and that his goodness was all that was required.

Once again, Jesus was showing everyone what the upside-down kingdom looked like. While everyone else would have honored Simon for his status and good practices, Jesus honored the woman for her need and submission. While Simon judged the woman and wrote her off, Jesus elevated her and forgave her sins. While the Pharisees relied on their own strength, actions, and practice, Jesus praised the unclean, scandalous woman because she knew how much she needed Jesus's forgiveness.

Luke 8:1–3. A group of wealthy women went along with Jesus and his disciples on his preaching tour in the region of Galilee. It was not unusual for cult leaders, psychics, or other traveling men in the ancient world to have female benefactors, but these women were not just giving their money. He had healed them of terrible afflictions, and out of their gratitude, they provided for his material needs and became his traveling companions. While the rabbis refused to teach women, considering them inferior, Jesus included them as vital parts of the community that served and ministered with him.

Luke 8:4–15. Most parables are stories with an obvious meaning and a not-so-obvious, hidden meaning. The enormous crowds that were listening to Jesus at this point came with mixed motives: genuine seekers of the coming Messiah, those who thought Jesus might be the next political power, those who wanted healing, and those who simply came to see what the fuss was all about. Parables were the method he used to distinguish the genuine seekers from the thousands of others. All four types of "soil" would have been represented in the large crowd to which he was speaking.

What Jesus means by "secrets" in verse 9 is an understanding of the kingdom that must be revealed by God himself. Jesus laid out the meaning of the parable for his disciples. The seed is God's Word, and it is the condition of the soil that matters. God's Word in rich soil has far greater yields. The fruit borne by the good soil is obedience to God's Word over the long haul, discipleship with perseverance—not perfect discipleship, but a fruit-bearing life.

Luke 8:16–21. The description Jesus gives of the lamp continues the theme of the sower, encouraging us again to be rich soil. Our receptivity to the teaching he has already given us determines whether or not he chooses to reveal more to us.

It may seem in verses 19–21 that Jesus was denying his family or being cruel to them, but he was not telling us he didn't love his family. He was showing us that God's kingdom came before everything else. Those who shared this belief were even closer to him than his earthly family.

Luke 8:22–25. Some of these men were fishermen. They had seen a storm or two. But this storm scared them. Jesus was exhausted, and while the storm raged and water began to fill the boat, he slept on. The disciples had seen enough of Jesus to know they needed him, so they woke him. "We are perishing!" they said. Jesus then rebuked the elements. And it was calm. Just like that. The word of this man, Jesus, had stopped the violent storm. Then the real fear started, as they considered the power not of the storm but of the one standing in their boat.

"Who then is this?" they asked each other. This is the central question of Luke. Who is this man? Is he the Messiah? The anointed one to come? But we thought he would come and overthrow the government with his power. We thought he would lead an army that trampled every other. We thought we would see condemnation of all but the Jews. This Jesus is not doing any of these things. But he is the one who heals diseases, exorcises demons, and raises widows' sons from the dead. He tells stories that make it harder to follow him, not easier. He puts obedience to God even above loyalty to family. And the wind and waves listen to his word.

Luke 8:26–39. Jesus and his disciples came out of the storm and had barely stepped on land when a tortured man possessed by many demons met them. Notice that the demons clearly answered the question the disciples had asked in the boat. Who was Jesus? Jesus was the Son of the Most High God. The demons knew Jesus could do what he wanted with them. Just as the wind and waves had to obey Jesus's word, so did the demons.

The people of the region reacted in fear just like the disciples had when Jesus calmed the storm. Instead of welcoming the one who set their fellow human free, they asked him to leave. The freed man, on the other hand, wanted to stay near Jesus. His love and gratitude probably equaled that of the others Jesus had healed. But Jesus's call to the man was this: "Return home and tell how much God has done for you." Jesus had been careful on the other side of the lake not to declare his identity directly. But for this Gentile man, freed from the torture of Satan, he laid it out plainly.

Luke 8:40–56. Jesus's display of power and authority was not over. He returned from his trip across the lake to a waiting crowd. From within the crowd came Jairus, a ruler of the synagogue. His only daughter was dying. This distinguished man humbled himself before Jesus, got on his knees, and begged. Like the demons, like the man who had been healed, this father came in desperation. In moments of real need, there is no better place to be than begging before Jesus.

Meanwhile, a woman was sneaking through the crowd. She had been bleeding for twelve years, and according to Jewish ceremonial law, she was unclean. She had probably been living an isolated life along with physical pain. She believed if she could just touch Jesus she had a chance of being healed.

Suddenly Jesus felt something. The woman had probably touched the tassel that was attached to the corner of the garment he was wearing, which would have been reachable without his knowledge. Immediately she was healed. But Jesus would not let her slip away in the same way she had snuck toward him. He began calling her out, not because he didn't know who she was or what had happened, but because he wanted to restore her. This woman was physically healed, but she needed more than that and Jesus knew it. She needed to be restored to community and freedom. Jesus made her testify to her cleanness in front of everyone. Not only that, he dignified her by calling her daughter. Far from being secondary or patronized by Jesus, the women he met were honored, called to service, and treated with respect.

Back to Jairus's daughter. It was too late; she was dead. Or so it seemed. Jesus reassured the distraught father, requiring him to "only believe." All of the emotion must have swept over the father as he entered the house. There was his only daughter, lying motionless on her deathbed. Jesus touched her. This was the second time in the span of only a few minutes that he had become unclean. According to Jewish law, touching a dead body was even worse than touching a bleeding woman. But, Jesus was about to make the girl clean. The power of Jesus and his word was again on display: "Child, arise." In that moment, the spirit that had left her young body returned.

As he had done over and over, he told the parents to keep quiet about what had happened. But those around him were seeing the power of God through Jesus. His power was on display everywhere he went. He had raised multiple people from the dead, cast out demons, and calmed a storm. All of this he did with his word. He only needed to speak for things to happen.

See this king of heaven as he looked upon his generation with compassion. The centurion, the widow who lost her son, the woman who washed his feet with her hair while the proud Simon scoffed, the bleeding woman in the crowd—all received his compassion. This one who spoke to the sea and the storm came for the hurting women and the needy centurion. He came to die, to rise, to reign. He came to love us, the servant king.

Reflection Questions

5. The stories of Jesus healing a centurion's servant and raising a widow's son show the Son of God touching, entering in, healing, and being in the pain with his people. What from these accounts of Jesus have you personally experienced in your own life? What parts do you long to experience?

6. In the scene at Simon's house we see two very different reactions to the same Jesus. Why do you think that is? Of the two, which reaction does your heart more regularly have to Jesus? Why?

7. What do you find interesting or surprising about the list of women traveling with Jesus? Why?

8. Jesus's healing of the demon-possessed man exposes to us the battle going on in the spiritual realm that we often do not see. What about that makes you uncomfortable or confused?

9. All that was needed to heal Jairus's daughter was Jesus's word, but he used touch also. What does this teach us about God's desire to enter in physical, present ways? How does that convict you?

Focus verse: *And they went and woke him, saying, "Master, Master, we are perishing!" And he awoke and rebuked the wind and the raging waves, and they ceased, and there was a calm. He said to them, "Where is your faith?" And they were afraid, and they marveled, saying to one another, "Who then is this, that he commands even winds and water, and they obey him?"*
Luke 8:24–25

Reflections, curiosities, frustrations:

Study 4

The Subversive King

Read Luke 9

Observation Questions

1. What were Jesus's instructions to the apostles when he sent them out in Luke 9:1–6?

2. Describe the details of what happened at the feeding of the five thousand (Luke 9:10–17).

3. In Luke 9:18–22 what were the different things people were saying about who Jesus was? Who did Peter say he was? What was Jesus's response to this?

4. What was Jesus's response when someone said that they would follow him wherever he went (Luke 9:57)?

Luke 9:1–3. For months the disciples had listened to Jesus's teaching, watched him heal the crowds, and followed him to new villages and across the water. The time to simply observe was over. The power the disciples had watched Jesus wield he now gave to them, along with the authority to use it. This was their initiation into the ministry of the kingdom. Now they would do what Jesus had done. His mission became their mission. Their charge was to proclaim the kingdom and to heal, to attend to both the soul and the body. This sending was also to prepare the disciples for teaching and making disciples after Jesus's death. These twelve men could not have imagined such a calling at this point. But Jesus, who always equips his children for their roles in his work, was preparing them even now.

The phrase "he sent" in verse 2 is a form of the verb *apostellō*, from which we get the word *apostle*. These apostles were the sent ones. Apparently there were many who went from town to town, sometimes making a decent living by collecting money in exchange for their proclamations and ideas. Unlike the traveling preachers who were their contemporaries, the disciples were to rely on God to meet their needs. Jesus was teaching them to trust, to expect God to provide. This is different from future trips where he would instruct them to take provisions. For this particular, inaugural mission, they were to rely completely on the hospitality of fellow Jews, prepared by God to receive them.

Luke 9:4-6. The house that rejected the disciples' message essentially rejected Jesus, and therefore the kingdom. Thus, judgment was coming for them. As a sign of this judgment, the disciples were to shake the dust of that town from their feet, a reference to the practice of some Jews removing the dust from their sandals when they returned from ceremonially unclean Gentile areas. And so they went from village to village, preaching and healing, spreading the news of the kingdom.

Luke 9:7-9. Jesus's growing popularity felt like a threat to the local Roman authority, Herod. The rumors that were circulating about Jesus left Herod confused, feeling threatened by Jesus's growing following but also curious and hoping to see Jesus for himself. His question echoes the one the disciples asked about Jesus after the storm: "Who is this about whom I hear such things?" Everyone who encounters Jesus eventually has to answer this question.

Who is Jesus? There is no neutral answer. No house could remain undecided about the ministry of the apostles. They either received them and supported their ministry or rejected them and faced God's judgement. The same is true today. No one is neutral before the king who sent out the twelve disciples. We are either for him or against him, his ally or his enemy.

Luke 9:10–17. The disciples returned from their first mission trip, probably worn out and full of stories and questions. Jesus took them to a quiet place to rest and regroup, but the crowds, always in need, followed him. Notice that he welcomed them. They were not an interruption or an annoyance, though his intention was to be alone with the disciples. God incarnate is not put off by our need. Rather, he welcomes it.

As it got late in the day, the people were getting hungry. They were in a deserted place, and the disciples' natural response was to send everyone away to get their own dinner. But Jesus was beginning to teach his followers how to live a life of dependence on him. Everything they needed for the crowd was standing before them. But these disciples did not yet understand the fullness of Jesus's identity.

Jesus's generous provision in this miraculous meal echoed God's provision for the Israelites in the wilderness; it also foreshadowed the Lord's Supper, which then foretells the coming messianic banquet. Here was a glimpse of the bounty, provision, and sweetness of Jesus's rule. Everyone had all they needed to be satisfied.

Luke 9:18–27. Months of teaching and ministry had led to this moment where the disciples, with Peter as their spokesperson, finally got it right. When Jesus asked them who they thought he was, Peter answered plainly, "The Christ of God." One would think that from this point on the disciples would have been fully in step with Jesus's ministry. Unfortunately, while they understood he was the Christ, the anointed one, they did not yet understand the nature of this role. When he told his disciples that he would suffer and be killed, Jesus was correcting their expectations of what the Christ had come to do.

Jesus's explanation of his mission also had implications for his disciples. If they were going to follow him, their lives needed to take the same shape as his. He was asking them to give up control of their lives, make a commitment that would lead to rejection, and travel with him as he made his eventual way to Jerusalem to die.

Luke 9:28–36. Jesus had gone to a secluded place to pray, and in the midst of his communion with God, his glory broke through in a dazzling display. Two men were with Jesus, Moses and Elijah. Moses points us to the past, while Elijah points us to the future. Moses led the Israelites out of Egypt in the Exodus. He was a type, a foreshadowing of Jesus, who would lead all of God's people out of the bondage of sin. In fact, in verse 31, the word translated as "departure" is *exodon*, which literally means "exodus." Jesus, Moses, and Elijah were talking about the exodus that Jesus was going to accomplish when he went to Jerusalem. Elijah points us to the future, the eschaton, the end of the world. There will be a final exodus, when all of God's people will be led out of the broken world and the bondage of sin, into a new heaven and new earth. All of this was about to be secured by Jesus.

Peter's desire to treat Jesus, Moses, and Elijah as equals with three equal shelters revealed that he still did not grasp the unique, elevated status of Jesus.[1] Jesus was not equal with anyone but God.

Luke 9:37–43. Why was Jesus upset? Recall Luke 9:1: "And he called the twelve together and gave them power and authority over all demons and to cure diseases…" All demons. The disciples had the power. They had the authority. They even had the experience. In Matthew's account of this interaction, Jesus explains to his disciples that they couldn't cast out this demon "Because of [their] little faith" (Matthew 17:20). He had given them authority and power. They did not believe him. This brings a harsh rebuke from Jesus.

---

[1] Robert H. Stein, *Luke: An Exegetical and Theological Exposition of Holy Scripture*, vol. 24 of New American Bible Commentary, New Testament Set Book Series (Nashville, TN: Holman Reference, 1993), 285.

Luke 9:44-50. While the disciples were still marveling at the deliverance from the demon, Jesus commanded their attention with what must have seemed like confusing and foreign words: "The Son of Man is about to be delivered into the hands of men." Not "the Messiah is about to triumph" or "the Christ will soon upset the current balance of power." Instead, he was saying the one they had come to believe was the savior from God was about to be given by God to those who want to destroy him. He was once again shaping their understanding of the nature of the Messiah. But they did not understand, as evidenced by their behavior that followed: they began to argue about who was the greatest.

Jesus flipped the disciples' distorted view of greatness on its head. Greatness is different in Jesus's kingdom: it is not in exaltation of self but in exaltation of others; it is not in gaining the world but in losing it.

Luke 9:51-56. The days of traveling around Galilee preaching and teaching were over. Jesus was transitioning to a new phase of ministry. He would be resurrected, but first he must be killed. Lest we think he was only a victim and not a willing participant, we must remember these words. He set his face to go to Jerusalem. He chose. He accepted, determined, and resolved. Jesus died on purpose. For you.

It is hard to overestimate the amount of hatred between Jews and Samaritans. Their disagreements with the Jews were so severe that Samaritans would not extend the cultural norm of hospitality for anyone journeying to Jerusalem for worship. There are even historical accounts of Samaritans murdering Jews attempting to make this pilgrimage to Jerusalem. The disciples wanted instant judgment for the Samaritan village, immediate retribution for rejecting Jesus. But Jesus wanted to give them time. He displays the same patience with us today. He gives us multiple opportunities to hear the gospel and graciously delays his judgment.

Luke 9:57–62. Jesus never downplayed the cost of discipleship. His reply to this first would-be disciple revealed just one of many places where his followers would have to give up any certainty of comfort; even a place to sleep at night was not guaranteed.

Jesus's reply to the next person was even more shocking. Burying a father was the highest duty for a Jew; only fulfilling a Nazirite vow or acting as the high priest took precedence over it.[2] But Jesus was making it clear that the kingdom must always be the highest priority. He was making a play on words here. Obviously someone who is already dead cannot bury someone else. Jesus meant that the spiritually dead can bury their own physically dead. Those who had no part in the kingdom could do these tasks. But disciples could not employ this excuse for disobedience. They must not delay in what Jesus asks them to do, but instead they must comply with Jesus's will when and where he asked.

For the third man, Jesus uses an illustration. A farmer needed to guide the plow with his left hand while prodding the oxen with his right. If he turned to look back, the furrow he was attempting to create for planting crops would be crooked. For Jesus, there was no acceptable "I will follow you, but..." statement. It was not that he was or is opposed to us fulfilling earthly duties. Instead, he was making clear the fact that the kingdom of God must be our first concern and paradigm for all decisions.

The king of heaven had again shown his glory by feeding a crowd of five thousand from a small lunch and showing his supernatural brightness to a few on the mountain. But the true Messiah would suffer, and Jesus set his face toward Jerusalem to do so. All who would follow him must count the cost of their decision. He came to die, to rise, to reign. He came to love us, the servant king.

---

[2] Stein, *Luke*, 301.

Reflection Questions

5. Herod asks a question we all have to ask ourselves: Who is this Jesus, and how do we respond to him? Who do you say he is? Why?

6. Jesus begins to reveal to the disciples that life is about dependency on him and his ability to satisfy the layers of human need. Where are you currently resisting dependency on Jesus? How can you begin to talk with him about it?

7. Jesus was starting to reshape their ideas of what the Christ had come to do and how he would do it, living a life that would lead to self-denial, suffering, and ultimately death. What did this "take up his cross daily and follow me" mean for the disciples? What does it mean for you today?

8. After Jesus foretells his death, the disciples get into an argument over who is the greatest among them. Where are you currently struggling in a similar way with status or grasping for power when it comes to your service to God and to his people?

9. Jesus tells the disciples that the kingdom of God must be the highest priority. How does this call intimidate you? How does it give you joy?

Focus verse: *And he called the twelve together and gave them power and authority over all demons and to cure diseases, and he sent them out to proclaim the kingdom of God and to heal.*
Luke 9:1–2

Reflections, curiosities, frustrations:

Study 5

The Praying King

Read Luke 10–11

Observation Questions

1. List all the details in the parable of the Good Samaritan (Luke 10:25-37).

2. Describe what happens when Jesus interacts with Martha and Mary (Luke 10:38-42).

3. After Jesus casts out a demon, what conversation does he have with those around him watching what just occurred (Luke 11:14-23)?

4. In Luke 11:37-52, when speaking with the Pharisees and the lawyers, Jesus says the word "woe" six times. List all the reasons for his "woes."

Luke 10:1–12. These disciples were being commissioned by the Son of God to teach and supernaturally heal. These were not the original twelve disciples but additional men, giving us a picture of the number of people who at this point had attached themselves to Jesus.

Jesus sent them with a sense of urgency: they were not to take extra sandals but to get up and go; they were to rely on the hospitality of the people they met; they were not to worry about Jewish food laws but to eat whatever was set before them; they were to keep moving rather than engaging in lengthy greetings along the road. They were to preach and demonstrate the nearness of the kingdom of God.

Luke 10:13-16. These are declarations of sadness, disappointment, anguish, and mourning by Jesus. He wishes not for judgment but for repentance. He knows that judgment is coming and that it will be more severe for those cities who had actually seen and heard him; they would be held responsible for what they had seen and yet rejected. Many of us have had years of Bible study, sermons, and other teaching from the Word of God. We are rich with resources and opportunities to understand who Jesus is. Because of this, we will be judged more harshly if we reject him. On the other hand, if we live in submission to Christ, not perfectly, but faithfully, we will find ourselves hungering for more of him, his Word, and his way (and he will perfectly and faithfully satisfy this hunger). Whether we have followed him for years or are just now realizing the wealth of exposure we've been given, we must repent, for the kingdom of heaven is at hand.

Luke 10:17-20. The seventy-two had experienced the power of Jesus's name. They were inspired, propelled by the work God had done through them. When we see God's power and authority working amidst the broken, hopeless futility of this world, it is exhilarating.

Jesus's point is not so much that his followers can touch and handle snakes and scorpions—traditionally used as symbols of evil—without threat of danger. Instead, he is declaring that the powers they represent can and will be crushed. Victory is certain for the disciples of Jesus.

In the middle of the disciples' joy and celebration, Jesus tells them this victory pointed ultimately to something greater, something of lasting joy. The word translated "are written" means to inscribe or enter in a public register, like a census. Jesus is telling them that their names have been entered into the registry of heaven. It cannot be altered; it will not be lost. This, says Jesus, is something to celebrate.

Luke 10:21-24. It gave Jesus pleasure not only that his Father chose to give the gift of salvation but also that he disclosed it in the way that he did. It was not given on the basis of wisdom, status, intelligence, or power. It was not first offered to the learned or the proud. Instead, it was given to the lowly, the common, those who were no more than babes. What an upside-down distribution of understanding. What an unexpected way to multiply his mission and advertise his message. Generations had longed for this moment, when Jesus would finally be revealed as the one true king. But God chose to give this epiphany to the humble, the average, the simple-minded. This is the upside-down kingdom, where God reveals himself in the weakness of ordinary humans.

Luke 10:25-37. This lawyer was using a litmus test for Jesus's orthodoxy. Jesus answered his question with a question, something that made the expert uncomfortable. The lawyer knew the correct answer, as any devout Jew would have repeated the two texts he quoted (Deuteronomy 6:5 and Leviticus 19:18) twice per day. Their discussion could have ended there, but the lawyer wanted to justify himself, to prove his righteousness. He wanted Jesus to say the scope of his responsibility was limited. Jesus answered with a story that illustrated a life of costly love.

Though the abused traveler was unnamed, the hearers would have assumed he was a Jew. While Jews were usually not supposed to come into contact with dead or unclean bodies, all Jewish law prioritized the saving of a life. Even if the man were dead, Jewish law demanded a proper burial. Thus, the first two men—a priest and then a Levite, a descendant from the priestly family of Aaron—had no excuse for passing by. Jesus shocked his listeners by inserting a hated Samaritan as the hero.

The priest and Levite distanced themselves from the trouble and pain of the injured man, while the Samaritan had compassion and used what resources he had to show mercy and reduce the pain and danger of the wounded man. Again and again the Samaritan gave in abundance to his enemy—not based on his worthiness, but based on his need.

Luke 10:38-42. Mary was sitting at the feet of Jesus, the proper place for a disciple, though not usually for a woman; normally only men were allowed to learn from a rabbi. Mary chose the "good portion," literally the "good part." Of course, the things Martha was doing were important. Martha was not doing something wrong in serving, but she was preoccupied by her tasks and was therefore missing the good part—the opportunity to sit at Jesus's feet and hear his words.

Luke 11:1-4. Jesus had stepped aside to pray again. Over and over the disciples had seen him pull himself away from everyone and pray. He was praying before the dove descended on him during his baptism. He prayed all night before choosing the disciples. He was praying when they went ahead in the boat across the lake. He took Peter, John, and James up on the mountain to pray just before the Transfiguration. Luke 5:16 tells us that Jesus frequently withdrew into the wilderness to pray.

This is actually the only time recorded in the gospel that the disciples asked Jesus to teach them anything. What he gave them was not a formula or a rosary but a guide. He probably did not mean for them merely to repeat the words by rote but to provide a paradigm for prayer. The gist of it was this: God's glory and his kingdom must be our first desire. We live in utter dependence upon him. This is not only the way to pray but the way to live. This is the way of discipleship.

The prayer starts with a desire for all to worship God as he should be worshipped, to honor him as he should be honored, to come to him in the posture of obedience and adoration that he deserves. When God's glory is not our first and deepest longing, this is the place to stop, realign ourselves with reality, and ask the Lord to make it so.

The next petition is for God's kingdom to come. We are asking for more people to live in obedience to the good king. We ask that the kingdom that was inaugurated by Jesus's earthly ministry be extended and enlarged by the Holy Spirit.

Everything we need for every day in this world comes from the Father. Just as we require food and other necessities daily, we also need to confess our sins and extend forgiveness to others daily.

The fourth petition, about temptation, is not a request for rescue from every trial. Rather, we ask God to keep us away from things that might lead us to destruction, to walking away from him altogether, to abandoning our faith.

Luke 11:5-10. This story is an illustration of contrast, meant to encourage us to pray. If this sleeping, reluctant man responds to the needs of his friend because of his rude persistence, how much more will the always-attuned, kind Father respond to the needs of his children? God does not need to be convinced or roused. Our Father listens for our voice; he waits to hear from us.

Luke 11:11-13. God only gives good things, like the Holy Spirit, who is the Comforter, the Counselor, the one who attends us at every moment. There are things that we know are invariably good—salvation and growth in grace, both for us and others. But other things are not so simply discerned as good or evil. How could it be bad to ask for a promotion or for a loved one to live or for God to provide in a certain way? But in our limited perception, we may unknowingly ask for things that will tempt, harm, or lead us astray. God will only give us things that are for our good, our ultimate good, the good of our souls and our dependence and love for our Father.

Luke 11:14-23. Jesus explains why it was illogical to say, as some were, that he was using Satan's power. No, Jesus drove out demons by the power of God. Satan is the strong man in Jesus's parable. But, thanks be to God, he is not the strongest man. Satan has been defeated by the stronger one, Jesus. Jesus does not mince words about these two kingdoms. If you are not working for his kingdom, you are working against him.

Luke 11:24-28. Jesus's story here teaches that good behavior is not salvation. The man has cleaned up his life, made some good choices, but the void left by the demon has not been filled by the Holy Spirit. In other words, this is a superficial change, not a spiritual transformation.

A woman in the crowd, in her joy and pleasure at what she hears, cries out a blessing on Jesus's mother. But Jesus points her to the greater good: true and deep contentment that comes from faithful obedience to his Word. May this be how we find our contentment, as we pray the way he taught us, are encouraged by his words to keep on praying, and live in hope while we wait for Jesus's kingdom to come.

Luke 11:29-32. Though there had been many signs—healings, feeding the five thousand, driving out demons—the skeptics wanted more. But Jesus knew it was not signs they needed but faith. He denied them any more signs except the future sign of Jonah. Just as Jonah was buried in the whale for three days and then emerged, so Jesus would be buried in the tomb for three days and then emerge.

When Solomon was king, the queen of Sheba journeyed more than a thousand miles to see if what she had heard about his riches and amazing wisdom was true (read 1 Kings 10:1-13). She declared God's glory and blessed him for his love for Israel. The people of Jesus's day saw more of God's wisdom in Jesus than the queen saw in Solomon, and yet their hard hearts refused to see God, though he was standing right in front of them. For this they would be judged.

Luke 11:33-36. Jesus, elsewhere called the Light of the World (John 8:12), was the lamp who shone the light of the gospel through his teaching and miracles. But it was the responsibility of the hearer to perceive and respond to Jesus's message. We, too, will be held accountable for our response to the amount of light we have received.

Luke 11:37-41. The Pharisees' ritual washing of hands was not a hygiene practice; it was a rite to decontaminate themselves from contact with sinners, a practice not prescribed by the Old Testament but rather recommended by their oral tradition.[1] Jesus called these hypocrites out. While seemingly clean on the outside, they were full of filth on the inside. This was an outward show, able to be done with a totally rotten heart. Jesus said that instead of these empty, outward displays, they should deal with the greed and wickedness on their insides.

Luke 11:37-44. The rest of Luke 11 contains six woes, expressions of "How terrible!" for the Pharisees. First, their tithing practice made a mockery out of what was supposed to be an outflow of their love for God and others. Next, they insisted on public acclaim instead of laying down their lives for others. Third, they painstakingly followed hundreds of laws so that they would never be ceremonially unclean, but they were spiritually unclean and therefore leading others to death.

---

[1] Leon Morris, *Luke*, Tyndale New Testament Commentaries (Downers Grove, IL: Intervarsity Press, 1974), 221.

The Pharisees formed as a group about 150 years earlier to learn the law in minute detail. They tried to simplify the law into manageable principles and practices that people could keep. There were two problems with this. First, they focused exclusively on external matters that ignored deeper, spiritual issues. They were scrupulous to "tithe mint and rue and every herb," but then they would "neglect justice and the love of God" (verse 42). We should remember that Jesus criticized the Pharisees for relaxing the law, not for making the law more strict (see Matthew 5:19–20). Second, by their attempts to "simplify" the law, they only ended up obscuring God's law by making it increasingly complex. They did not lift a finger to help the people keep the law, but only hindered others from entering the kingdom.

Luke 11:45–54. Lawyers were vocationally religious people, experts in the study of the Torah. They received Jesus's last three woes. First, they made serving God impossible for the average person. Second, they honored the dead prophets while ignoring their message. Finally, they covered up the essential meaning of God's Word. They distilled the account of the creator God's love for his people down to a list to be kept. Not only did they fail to enter the kingdom; they made it hard for others to enter.

From this point on in the Book of Luke, the scribes and Pharisees looked for a way to trap Jesus. They wanted a serious accusation that would hold up in their court, that they might condemn him. This is where a hard heart led them.

Again and again Jesus surprised those who listened to him. The seventy-two were to be overjoyed not at their ability but that their names were in the book of life. The cunning lawyer was to love his enemies like the Good Samaritan. The disciples were to pray as Jesus taught them, simply and as needy children, like the desperate friend at midnight. The Pharisees were rebuked again and again. This king of heaven surprised his listeners, and still surprises us if we're listening. He came to die, to rise, to reign. He came to love us, the servant king.

Reflection Questions

5. In the parable of the Good Samaritan, the priest and the Levite look away from the need of the injured man. Who in your household, workplace, community, or country have you been looking away from? Why?

6. Are you surprised that Jesus used a story of a man shamelessly begging to demonstrate what prayer should be like? How will that reshape the way you pray?

7. Jesus explains that when we pray to God, our good Father, he will give us good things, even if in our limited understanding we don't view them as good. What in your life story makes you struggle to believe this truth? Where do you need God to restore your view of him as a good Father?

8. Jesus redefines blessedness as less about familial connection and more about having a faith in God's Word that leads to action. How does this change your view of what it means to be blessed?

9. What started out as the Pharisees' attempt to perfectly follow the law went off the rails into blind legalism. Have you ever had a similar experience with legalism in your walk with the Lord? Describe what happened.

Study 5: The Praying King (Luke 10–11)

Focus verse: *"Which of these three, do you think, proved to be a neighbor to the man who fell among the robbers?" He said, "The one who showed him mercy." And Jesus said to him, "You go, and do likewise."*
Luke 10:36-37

Reflections, curiosities, frustrations:

Study 6

The Confrontational King

Read Luke 12–13

Observation Questions

1. In Luke 12:22-34, what does Jesus tell his disciples not to be anxious about?

2. List the details Jesus gives in Luke 12:35-48 about the various behaviors that the servants have while waiting for their master to return. What does Jesus say will happen to each of them?

3. What are the two things to which Jesus compares the kingdom of God in Luke 13:18-21?

4. In Luke 13:26–30, what does Jesus say his response will be to people who think proximity to him is the same as knowing him? Who will be in the kingdom of God instead?

Luke 12:1-3. Jesus's words here, though certainly overheard by the crowd, were for the disciples. In these last few months of his life, he was preparing his disciples for what was coming: rejection, persecution, grief, death threats, danger, need, and loss. Jesus knew what was ahead for these dear disciples, and he knows what is ahead for us.

Most people baked their own bread every day, and they would have pictured a small lump of dough that slowly grows as the leaven works its way through. The "leaven" of the Pharisees that would work its way through any group of people was that quiet temptation to be one person in public and another in private, to speak certain words in front of a group but then whisper what you really believe behind closed doors. Jesus warns that on Judgment Day, all our hidden words and actions will be brought out into the light.

Luke 12:4-7. Jesus spoke candidly about hell, not as a concept, but as a real place where real people go. But Jesus is speaking here to his dear ones, his friends, as he calls them. And while God has the power to put people in hell, he uses his immense power and infinite knowledge for the good of those who love him. God knows every person on the earth more intimately than they know themselves, and all of this knowledge he uses for their ultimate good.

Luke 12:8-10. These verses have caused many believers unneeded anxiety. Unlike Peter, who later in his life denied Jesus multiple times and then was restored, Judas is a better illustration of this type of denial, as one who never returned to Jesus. Blasphemy of the Holy Spirit is calling what is good evil, attributing to Satan what God has done. It is a permanent decision to reject Jesus. Believers who are living repentant lives and relying on Jesus for their righteousness need not fear that they will accidentally stumble into this sin.

Luke 12:11-12. Jesus reassures his disciples that the Holy Spirit would give them words in the exact moment they needed them so that the gospel might be proclaimed. He would tell them what to say so that the kingdom would advance.

Luke 12:13-21. Instead of deciding the case, Jesus went for the heart, speaking to the man's motivation—greed. The core of the story was this: the man relied on his wealth, not on God. For Western Christians living in affluence, there is a constant temptation to trust that we will be comfortable and taken care of because of our bank accounts, high-paying jobs, or inheritance. It is not the possessions or money that are faulty but our white-knuckled grasp on them and our trust in them instead of in God.

Luke 12:22–34. God's servants will have what they need. Jesus made this clear. Seek the blessings of heaven rather than the possessions of earth, he says. We need not fear; God is delighted to give us the kingdom itself. Our possessions are not given to us only for us, and when we give to others' needs, we are creating for ourselves some sort of "storehouse of wealth," as it could be translated, that goes beyond the grave. This kind of stash doesn't grow old, get stolen, or lose its value. Investments on this earth can provide small returns for, at best, eighty or ninety years. Investments in the kingdom provide returns that never end.

But Jesus gives us the most important reason to stockpile treasure in heaven: our hearts follow our money. If our largest and most consistent investments are in our beautiful houses, our travel, our children, or anything other than the kingdom, guess where our hearts will be? But if our investments are in building the kingdom of God, our hearts will follow.

Luke 12:35–40. Jesus's growing band of true followers spent days, months, even years with him as he taught and healed people. But he knew the time was coming when he would be gone and they would face intense struggle. He told them stories about what it means to be ready for him to return and to care for his people while they waited. We, too, live in between Jesus's first and second coming. And so his words instruct us as we wait for him.

The servants in the story were alert, prepared to open the door the moment their master arrived. In the same way, Jesus wants us to be ready at all times for his return, to be expectant and eager for his coming. For those whom the master finds awake and ready, a fabulous surprise is coming. The master himself will serve the servant. What a role reversal! Exactly when Jesus will come does not matter so much as the fact that he is coming. We must always be ready.

Luke 12:41-48. Jesus answers Peter's question with a story. When Jesus returns, those who are faithful with the knowledge and power they have been given will be rewarded with even more responsibility in his kingdom. But the opposite is also true. Those who are irresponsible with the knowledge and power they've been given will be punished. In fact, the person who abuses whatever or whomever is given to them to steward will be severely punished and put with the unfaithful because by their actions they show themselves to be unbelievers. This may seem like a harsh warning, but remember that Judas was among the disciples. These shocking words of Jesus were not directed toward pagans or the large crowds; they were spoken for his followers and his disciples. They were spoken for us. Jesus is not saying that those who fail in terrible ways can never find forgiveness; Peter denied Jesus multiple times and was restored. Instead, it is a warning that we are servants accountable to a master for how we act.

Luke 12:54-56. Jesus now turned his attention to the crowds, rebuking them for not also interpreting the signs of his teaching and miracles as they did the weather. These were the signs of God's redemption of Israel, spoken of by the prophet Isaiah (Isaiah 61). Jesus announced from the beginning of his ministry (Luke 4:18-19) that he had been anointed to preach good news to the poor, bring freedom for the prisoners, give sight to the blind, and release the oppressed. These were the very things he had been doing for three years in Galilee, clear signs of the kingdom of God. But the people did not see them for what they were because they did not want to.

Luke 12:57-59. These people understood their debts to each other, but Jesus was telling them that they completely misunderstood their account with him. They were, and we are, spiritually indebted to him because of our sin. We owe him an amount that is impossible to pay, leaving us only two choices: agree with God about the overwhelming debt and beg for mercy or refuse to repent and spend eternity paying.

Luke 13:1-5. The understanding of most first-century people was that bad things happened to bad people and good things to good people. Suffering was thought to be a result of personal sin. Recent tragedies had Jesus's listeners thinking that those who had been killed were probably more sinful than others and that their awful deaths were God's judgment. Jesus told them plainly that, no, those killed were not worse sinners than others. And then he directed them to the real question: What about you? The reality is that all people are sinful and deserving of bad things, so the question is, Will you die because of your sin, or will you repent and be saved from eternal death? Jesus often answered this way when people asked about the sin of others, turning the question around to make them face their own sin. He does the same for us today.

Luke 13:6-9. Israel had failed for some time to produce fruit. It was more than fair for the owner of the vineyard to give the command to cut down the tree when he found no fruit. The request for one more year is a picture of God showing his mercy and patience. The nation of Israel needed to respond quickly or face judgment. Though it is not the basis for his mercy or salvation, God always looks for fruit. We are not saved by our good works, but the good works we do are evidence of our salvation.

Luke 13:10-17. Jesus saw this woman, summoned her, and healed her. It was solely his compassion that initiated the act. He had come for people like her. But the ruler of the synagogue would not have it. Jesus, as usual, did not mince words. What was the true meaning of the Sabbath? To keep the regimented rules laid out by the Pharisees? No, Jesus was explaining. It was to "demonstrate the mercy of God," to give refreshment, rest, and healing. If anything, the Sabbath was the most appropriate day to heal.

Luke 13:18–21. The kingdom was already present in Jesus's ministry. In his teaching and healing, the kingdom had come. The healing of the bent-over woman was evidence of this. Though seemingly insignificant—one woman healed on one day—it signaled a beginning, a seed. A mustard seed was tiny, but the end result was huge. A little bit of leaven seemed unimportant but would permeate enough flour to make bread for one hundred people. The emphasis in these parables is not necessarily on the process of growth but on the contrast between the humble beginning and the dramatic end. This is how the kingdom works. It may look weak, feeble, and trivial at the beginning. It may be hidden, simple, easy to ignore. But the end result is remarkable, transformative, and inevitable.

Luke 13:22–27. Instead of a wide door welcoming the majority of Jews, Jesus was describing a narrow door through which many would not be able to pass and that would eventually close. Those outside the door would then begin to argue with Jesus, explaining their familiarity with him. But knowing Jesus as an acquaintance would not save anyone. In fact, unless their response to him was appropriate, Jesus says he would treat them like a stranger. The same danger exists for us today. We may assume that because of our familiarity with Jesus, the Bible, church, and religious activity, we will be saved. We may understand theological truths and even agree intellectually. But saving faith is not the same as head knowledge. Only recognition of our desperate need for Jesus's individual saving work in our lives will lead to entrance through the narrow door.

Luke 13:28–30. The "weeping and gnashing of teeth" would be signs of disappointment and frustration, a reaction to the shocking news that the religious leaders were wrong about their presumption of God's favor. This will be a picture of the first (the Jews, who expected to be a part of God's kingdom) being last and the last (the Gentiles, outsiders who did not expect to be in the kingdom) being first.

Luke 13:31–33. Herod thought he could simply kill Jesus and eliminate any risk of Jesus's popularity in Galilee. But Jesus had begun a mission when conceived by the Holy Spirit in the womb of his mother, Mary, that could not be stopped. He would go about his ministry exactly as he had planned. God, not Herod, would decide when and how Jesus would die. Jesus had set his face toward Jerusalem. This was a turning point in Jesus's journey, as he speaks like a prophet about Israel rejecting him. He knew what awaited him at the end of his road. He walked straight toward the suffering of Jerusalem, loving, teaching, and healing along the way.

Luke 13:33–34. Here we are privy to the lament of God over a city. See his longing, his ache. Hear the agony in his voice as he mourns their rejection. But Jerusalem, and much of Israel, would not accept him. They would not even acknowledge their need for a savior. They consistently refused to repent, despite God's care and offer of salvation.

As the king over every person everywhere, Jesus's authority would allow him to condemn and punish all of us outright. But as the generous, patient king of the upside-down kingdom, he offers to us what he offered to those along the road to Jerusalem: the opportunity to repent and find protection from the wrath of God that is coming. He invites us, he pleads with us, he longs for us to enter the narrow door by responding to his invitation to repent.

Jesus's teaching was difficult. He taught about hell, rebuked those who saved up for this world instead of the next, and told his followers to always be ready, not missing the signs right in front of them. He rebuked Israel for not producing fruit and lamented over the city of Jerusalem. But he also taught in parables about the kingdom, healed a woman on the Sabbath, and promised treasures that couldn't be lost. This king of heaven was nothing like the religious teachers of his day. He came to die, to rise, to reign. He came to love us, the servant king.

Reflection Questions

5. Instead of leading people to God, the Pharisees became a barrier to knowing him. When have you experienced this? When have you done this?

6. When you meditate on Jesus's words about our hearts following where we spend our money/treasure, what area of your own personal spending comes to mind? What would shifting to more kingdom investment look like practically?

7. How often do you think about or anticipate Jesus's promised return? What would readiness look like?

8. Jesus dismantles the popular belief of the day, and our current day, that good things happen to good people and bad things happen to bad people by demonstrating that all people are sinful, in need of saving. What part of this false belief have you held on to that you need to repent of?

9. After study and reflection on this passage in Luke, how do you see God's invitation and longing for us to repent? What questions does it leave you wrestling with for further study?

Focus verse: *"O Jerusalem, Jerusalem, the city that kills the prophets and stones those who are sent to it! How often would I have gathered your children together as a hen gathers her brood under her wings, and you were not willing! Behold, your house is forsaken. And I tell you, you will not see me until you say, 'Blessed is he who comes in the name of the Lord!'"*
Luke 13:34–35

Reflections, curiosities, frustrations:

Study 7

The Seeking King

Read Luke 14–16

Observation Questions

1. What are the details of what happened in the parable of the great banquet (Luke 14:12-24)?

2. What does Jesus say someone has to do to be his disciple (Luke 14:26-27)?

3. In the parable of the Prodigal Son, what did the younger son do and what was the father's response? What did the older son do and what was the father's response?

4. What happens in the story of the rich man and Lazaraus?

Luke 14:1–6. The Pharisees had set a trap for Jesus. They were watching him, waiting for him to make some theological error. They purposely placed a man with dropsy (a condition that caused swelling) right in front of Jesus. They counted on the fact that Jesus's compassion would lead him to heal the man on the Sabbath, but Jesus knew their hearts. Before healing the man, Jesus asked the lawyers and Pharisees whether it was lawful to heal on the Sabbath. If they answered yes, they would be going against their rabbinic teachings, since healing on the Sabbath was only allowed when life was in danger and this man surely could have been healed another day. If they said no, they might have been seen as cruel and inhumane. There was nothing in the Old Testament prohibiting healing on the Sabbath. Jesus's argument about kindness shown to children and animals on the Sabbath was irrefutable. He was showing them the true meaning of the Sabbath and the love of the one who created it.

Luke 14:7-11. Jesus was not only talking about table manners. His illustration was a description of what it looked like to follow him as king. This was kingdom etiquette—the promotion of others before self-promotion. What a profoundly different value system than that of the world, which so loudly reminds us to promote ourselves, put ourselves first, and make sure everyone understands our significance. Instead, Jesus teaches us that it is God's responsibility to improve our reputation. As a follower of Jesus, the way up is down, and exaltation is decided by the Lord, not by pushing our way to the top.

Luke 14:12-14. "Do not invite" could be better translated as "stop continually inviting."[1] Instead of only inviting people who could repay them their favor, Jesus told his listeners to invite those who could never reciprocate. Then, instead of their meal simply being repaid with a friend's meal, they would be repaid by God at the resurrection. But this was not just any group of people that Jesus was recommending the Pharisees invite. In Leviticus 21, God gave a list of those not allowed to go into God's sanctuary—the crippled, the blind, and the lame. The very same list of people Jesus named as those who should be invited. Something new was happening. Jesus was commanding that the excluded be included, for his sake.

Had God changed his mind about who could be in his presence? Was the law of God changing? Absolutely not. The requirements to be in the presence of God still stood. But now there was one who could do so perfectly. Because of Jesus's sinless life (and eventual death and resurrection), access was granted to God's presence for everyone, everywhere.

---

[1] Stein, *Luke*, 390.

Luke 14:15-24. Jesus had proclaimed the presence of the kingdom and offered an invitation to it over and over as he taught and healed in the synagogues. But the Jewish leaders repeatedly refused him. Instead of responding with repentance and faith, they tried to trap him. These men who believed they would have the best places at God's final banquet would fail to receive a seat there at all; their seats would be given to others. God's plan to fill his house would not be thwarted by the hard-hearted refusal of the Jews to respond to him. Instead, the Gentiles, the broken, and the second-class citizens would take their places at the feast. This is the great reversal. This is the upside-down kingdom.

Luke 14:25-33. At this point Jesus's words were chosen not for the Pharisees, nor for his disciples, but for the crowds. Discipleship has a cost, and Jesus wanted the crowds to carefully consider it before committing themselves to him. First, he told them, you must (comparatively) hate everyone else. Jesus was not instructing them to literally hate their families. Instead, their love for all others would so pale in comparison to their love for him that it would seem like hate. Disciples are still called to hold their relationship to Jesus above anyone else. We must depend on Jesus more than we depend on our best friend, husband, or mom. Our call is to seek his praise and pleasure above all, to make him our highest love.

Second, we must bear our own cross. Jesus was always referring to self-denial when he talked about the cross. Responding to Jesus's invitation means following him into suffering and servanthood. The disciple is not above his master, and the master was crucified.

Luke 14:33 offers the third entry requirement for Jesus's kingdom: renounce all that you have. This does not mean that all disciples are to give away or sell everything they have. Some were and still are called to such a life, but not most. This is a call to recognize who actually owns all things. We must always be aware that we are not owners but stewards of our money, our things, our family, and even our own bodies.

If we are at all aware of our own hearts, these requirements will feel impossible. Our selfish, prideful souls recoil at the thought of being rejected by our families. We want nothing to do with suffering or self-denial. And we certainly love to believe we are our own masters, free to direct our lives and resources for our own pleasure. Living lives of total surrender, willing to suffer and serve others at all times is impossible by our own wills. We cannot pay the cost of discipleship; we cannot afford to serve this king. But this is the upside-down kingdom. This is the servant king who loved us so much that he left the right hand of his Father for our sake. This king willingly bore his cross so that we would not have to.

Luke 14:34–35. If we are not useful, like salt that is not salty, we will be thrown out. There is no loitering in the kingdom of God. You are either an ally or an enemy, either building the kingdom or working against it.

Luke 15:1–2. Don't miss the last phrase of chapter 14: "He who has ears to hear, let him hear." Now read the very next verse, Luke 15:1. Who had ears to hear? The tax collectors and sinners. These were outsiders, unacceptable ones, second-class citizens in the eyes of the Jews. These were the people who regularly spent time with Jesus.

Our God is a God who loves to look for lost people. He does it willingly, eagerly, joyfully. And when he finds them, he cannot help but celebrate. This entire chapter demonstrates God's persistence while searching for spiritually lost people and his joy upon finding them.

Luke 15:3–7. Sheep are dumb animals and literally cannot survive without a shepherd. But searching for a missing sheep is not a perfunctory job done by an apathetic shepherd. This is an errand of joy. See the shepherd's delight at having found his lost sheep. He calls people together for a celebration. In the same way, God rejoices over a sinner who is brought back to him through Jesus, or through one of Jesus's disciples. "In heaven" is another way of talking about God. Our God throws a party when one sinner repents; that's how important each individual person is to him.

Luke 15:8-10. In losing one coin, this woman had lost one-tenth of her entire savings. When she finally found it, she, like the shepherd, called others together to rejoice with her. Jesus explained the parable with his description of God rejoicing over the sinner who repents. Seeing people turn away from their sin and to God fills him with gladness. It causes him to celebrate. The Pharisees and teachers of the law had no understanding of such joy. Instead, they were angry that Jesus associated with anyone unlike them. But Luke explains God's joy in seeking and finding the lost in order that we might share it and join him in it. Our evangelism can be motivated by the same joy. We are to seek the lost and find them with delight, just as God does.

Luke 15:11-19. For the younger son to ask for his share of the property was akin to telling his father, "I wish you were dead." But the father complied, and the younger son took what his father had earned and wasted it.

Confronted with both the end of his money and a famine, the younger son became so desperate that he began working with pigs, a job that was unthinkable for a Jew. It is often when we are in need and lonely that we come to our senses, finally aware of our true desperation. In this case the boy turned from his miserable, empty life with a full understanding of his guilt. He knew he had lost the right to be treated as a son, so he practiced a speech, hoping he could avoid his father's wrath and earn his way back to the position of a servant. This is the picture of repentance. There are no excuses, no explanations. The only thing the son brings to his father is his need and the hope of mercy.

Luke 15:20-24. Before he could even finish his speech, the father, who had run to greet him, covered him with kisses and affection. There was no punishment for the beloved son. Instead, the robe usually worn by a guest of honor was put on him. Sandals, which were not worn by servants or slaves but only by free men, were put on his feet. The calf that was being saved for some sort of special occasion was killed so that they might have a feast. The father was rejoicing, unable to contain his happiness. The day before, his son might as well have been dead, in a far country, lost to him. And now, against all hope, he had returned. The father was ecstatic. This is how God welcomes sinners, with joy and a party, with overwhelming happiness and a celebration.

Luke 15:25-32. We do not get any details about the relationship of the father and the older brother during the years when the younger brother was gone, but his reaction to his father's party tells us volumes about what had been going on in the older brother's heart.

The likeness of the older son to the Pharisees and scribes is unmistakable. He had no idea of the privilege he had been living under his entire life. He had no desire to associate with the shameful, irresponsible younger brother. He thought he had earned everything he had, was full of pride and self-righteousness, and disdained anyone who had not kept his standards. The great reversal was happening again: the younger son who was lost was now inside the party, while the older brother looked on from the outside. This same reversal was happening before the eyes of the crowds. The outsiders and sinners, who had ears to hear, were entering the kingdom, while Israel could only look on with anger and scorn. Through the parable, Jesus was quietly appealing even then to the Pharisees to come into the party. All that was needed was recognition of their need for a savior, given to them in Jesus.

Luke 16:1–9. This entire chapter can be understood if we first grasp one concept: stewardship. Everything we own belongs to God. We are simply stewards of our houses, our cars, our money, our mutual funds, even our bodies. God has given us temporary use of his things, and we act as managers of his possessions during our lifetimes. We must manage them according to Jesus's wisdom.

Jesus turned his attention to his disciples, telling them the story of the clever manager. The man was going to be fired. In the meantime, he schemed and planned. He assumed that by getting into favor with the debtors, he would make friends for himself who would help him when he no longer had a job. The master was commending not the immorality of the steward but his shrewdness. Jesus explained the parable this way: Unbelievers are sometimes more clever in planning for their future than believers. Just like the clever manager who planned for his future, sons of light (believers) must plan for their future—the wedding feast of the Lamb. They must wisely steward their possessions in anticipation of their eternity. This may sound like earning salvation by works, specifically by being a good steward; it is not. Jesus was speaking to believers here, those already saved through faith. Instead of teaching the way of salvation in this passage, Jesus was telling believers to be as shrewd in their scheming toward a heavenly future as unbelievers are in planning for their earthly futures. Their shrewdness should reflect a life of repentance and a heart that is bearing fruit.

Luke 16:10–13. Stewardship of small things is a litmus test for how one will handle big things. If we cannot wisely steward God's things on this earth, why would he give us true riches—possessions in heaven? We are either working toward the ultimate goal of possessing things here (which we can never really do) or there. We can either serve money or God, not both. We can either be concerned with the "now" of earthly riches or the "then" of heavenly reward.

Luke 16:14-18. The Pharisees regularly gave to the poor but did so in order to be seen by others and to have a good reputation in the community. The Pharisees and scribes loved the law more than anything, but if they had truly understood it, they would have used their wealth for those in need. People all around them were entering the kingdom while the Pharisees rejected Jesus again and again. If they really wanted to obey the law, they needed to fully embrace Jesus, to whom all of the law pointed. For none of the law, not even one of the tiny lines or dots that differentiated one Hebrew letter from another, would ever change, but all of it would be fulfilled in Christ.

Why did Jesus suddenly begin to teach about marriage and divorce? He was probably using it as an example of the way the law would not change. Rabbis regularly taught that a man could divorce his wife for petty things. Jesus's words name the law's original intention, that man and woman would remain one.

Luke 16:19-31. Jesus's teaching about stewardship continued in the parable of the rich man and Lazarus. Jesus reversed the expected order of things and gave the poor man a name, while the rich man remained nameless. Even more, the great reversal had taken place, as the one who had nothing on earth was rich in heaven, while he who had owned so much was in torment, fully conscious while enduring agony. Jesus's words from his great sermon were being fulfilled. Think back to his teaching in Luke 6:20-21 and 24-25. The great reversal of the upside-down kingdom had taken place.

This is not a story about a rich man going to hell because he was rich and a poor man going to heaven because he was poor.

The poor man received what everyone who repents of their sin and believes in Jesus will receive—life forever with God in a place of peace and joy. The rich man had been given huge amounts of money by God to steward while on earth. But his lack of compassion on Lazarus revealed a hard heart that had not repented. This is a stern warning to those of us to whom God has given any kind of wealth. We must always remember that we are only stewards and that we will one day answer to our master, the true owner.

Those who originally read Luke's gospel would have surely thought of Jesus's death and resurrection as they read verses 30 and 31. He had risen from the dead, and yet most of Israel did not believe. Those who had been the insiders, the nation of Israel, had become the outsiders, while the Gentiles (non-Israelites) had found their way into the kingdom. More of the great reversal was happening.

Jesus had set his face toward Jerusalem, teaching along the way, welcoming crowds, eating with tax collectors and sinners, and instructing his disciples. The kingdom of heaven was near, a party was being planned, and all were invited. The upside-down kingdom had come in Jesus Christ. His call to those who lived then was the same as his call to us now: Come, take up your cross, and follow me. He came to die, to rise, to reign. He came to love us, the servant king.

Reflection Questions

5. In Luke there are three accounts of Jesus healing on the Sabbath and facing the anger and resistance of the religious leaders. When have you wanted to be more "right" than merciful?

6. Discipleship is costly, requiring self-denial. What about this call feels hard to you?

7. What do the three parables in Luke 15 (the lost sheep, lost coin, and lost sons) reveal to us about God's heart for seeking out his lost children?

8. Stewardship is the job of supervising or taking care of something. It is less about what you have and don't have and more about what you do with what you have been given. As you reflect on this, how is the parable of the rich man and Lazarus calling you to repent?

9. The upside-down kingdom that Jesus is bringing is the great reversal. Religious status or wealth do not get you into heaven, only repentance and belief in Jesus can. How can you relate to trusting in false gospels and beliefs for your salvation instead of in the work of Jesus?

Focus verse: *"Just so, I tell you, there will be more joy in heaven over one sinner who repents than over ninety-nine righteous persons who need no repentance."*
Luke 15:7

Reflections, curiosities, frustrations:

Study 8

The Weeping King

Read Luke 17–19

Observation Questions

1. What are the things Jesus says about sin in Luke 17:1–4?

2. In Luke 17:20-21, when Jesus is speaking to the Pharisees, how does he describe the coming kingdom of God?

3. Compare the Pharisee's behavior and words with those of the tax collector in the temple in Luke 18:9-14. Who does Jesus say is justified in this parable? Why?

4. Describe what Jesus does as he enters Jerusalem (Luke 19:28-48).

Luke 17:1–6. Jesus turns his attention here to his disciples only. He first gives a warning about temptation. Things that tempt us to sin are all around us, but Jesus is particularly protective of new or fragile believers, "little ones." It would be better to have a stone tied around your neck and to drown than to face the consequences of causing one of them to stumble.

Next, Jesus comments about living in community as Christians. Inevitably we will sin against one another. Rather than retreating or stuffing our anger, Jesus commands us to rebuke those who sin against us. We confront that person in order that we might eventually forgive, just as our Father has done with us over and over.

Third, and perhaps in response to Jesus's command to forgive a brother so many times, the apostles ask for more faith. But

Jesus wants them to use the faith they already have. He explains it is not the amount of faith but the object of their faith that matters.

Luke 17:7–10. Servants don't earn special privileges by doing their job. The expectation for living under another's authority is consistent obedience. As believers we live under the authority of the Lord; we must adhere to his rules, his desires, his pattern. We are to serve the one who saved us in whatever ways he may demand.

Luke 17:11-14. The lepers Jesus encountered here would have had to keep a safe distance from anyone not infected with leprosy. They called out to Jesus, hoping to get his attention. They had heard that Jesus was someone who could help them, and their words have the feeling of urgency. These were desperate, lonely, isolated people who had enough faith to yell to a stranger who might have the power to help.

Jesus saw them and called for yet more faith. According to Old Testament law, in order for someone to be completely healed a priest had to certify the healing and declare them "clean." But Jesus was speaking to these men as if they'd already been healed. He was calling them to believe and walk in the direction of the priest. And as these men walked toward the priest, they were healed.

Luke 17:15–19. Imagine the joy and relief as these men discovered that their disease was gone, that the reason for their isolation, poverty, and suffering had been taken away. All ten of the men were given the miracle of healing, but only one considered the source. This man had made the connection: God was acting through the person in front of him, Jesus. His response was to worship.

Then Luke drops the bomb: The one who returned to give thanks was a Samaritan. The Jews had the law that spoke of him, the prophets that pointed to him, and the psalms that sang about him, but they missed Jesus. Only the Samaritan understood and worshipped appropriately.

The ingratitude of the other nine lepers shows us that people can be recipients of God's common grace—the good things God gives all of humanity—and still not really know or worship him. It seems that the thankful leper also received grace that saved him from everlasting death. Jesus said to him, "Your faith has made you well" (literally, "Your faith has saved you"). All ten men called for help from Jesus; all ten were healed as they walked toward the priest in faith; but only one was saved. Reception of God's gifts does not equal salvation.

Luke 17:20-21. The Pharisees had been surrounded by signs of the kingdom. Still, they could not see the kingdom's coming. Jesus told them, "The kingdom of God is in the midst of you." It is among you, near you. In fact, it is standing right in front of you. Here we have one of the most helpful doctrines of our faith: the already–not yet nature of the kingdom of God. It is already at work and present but not fully accomplished yet. Only at the end of time, when Jesus returns as king, will the kingdom be brought to a state of perfection and total fulfillment.

Luke 17:22–25. Jesus knew that a time would come after his death and resurrection that the disciples would wish to see him return. He knew that some would claim to have seen his return, but these would be futile announcements. His return, his actual return, would be seen by everyone, like lightning lighting up the entire sky. It will be impossible to miss the return of Jesus at the end of time; it will be no secret.

Luke 17:30–37. When Jesus comes a second time, it will be just as unexpected as the flood was for the people of Noah's day or the destruction of Sodom was in Lot's day. At that moment there will be no sense in trying to preserve one's life on earth. Jesus doesn't mince words when he talks about his second coming. We who are abiding in him have nothing to fear of this day but can anticipate joyful fellowship with our king. But we are surrounded by those for whom this will be an overwhelming shock, followed by the terrible realization that only misery is coming for them. It will be a gruesome time, full of death. The time to be sure we are on the side of Jesus is now. When that great day comes, it will be too late.

Luke 18:1-8. This is a continuation of the scene we left at the end of chapter 17. People will be living life as usual when Jesus suddenly returns, and we must be ready. Jesus tells a parable about praying as we wait. Specifically, he instructs the disciples in how to pray for justice. The widow pestered the judge, annoying him to the point that he responded only to be rid of her. This needy woman relentlessly asked a godless, hardened judge to grant justice. Jesus is instructing us to do the same of the only perfectly just judge. As we walk through suffering and wait in pain for Jesus's return, we must pray and not give up. We live in the already–not yet, between Jesus's first coming and his glorious second coming. While we wait, we must not stop asking for his justice, whether for ourselves or for some other powerless or oppressed person. Minorities, foster kids, refugees, the persecuted church, and a myriad of voiceless people come to mind. With these, we must live in dependence upon his justice while we wait.

Luke 18:9-17. These two men could not have been more different in their approaches to God. The Pharisee stood in the temple boasting about his own wonderful moral character, confident in his own actions. The tax collector begged God for mercy, which he knew he didn't deserve because of his own sin. Only one—the tax collector—walked away justified, forgiven, and with right standing before God. It is not our goodness or discipline that earns our justification; it is only God's mercy.

Luke 18:18–30. The ruler thought himself and his actions to be good enough. But Jesus pushed past the man's actions and into his idolatrous heart. Jesus wanted the man to depend on him, not his money. This was too much for the man, who went away sad. This is not a command for everyone who wants salvation to sell everything they own. This was a call for this specific man to put aside his idols and trust Jesus to meet his needs. Jesus wanted the young man's heart, his total trust. Jesus knew that the man's wealth was what was standing in the way, so he demanded that he lay it down.

Jesus is using hyperbole to make a point: Just as it is impossible, literally impossible, for a camel (the largest known living object at the time in the Near East) to go through the eye of a needle (the smallest hole known at the time), so it is impossible for a rich person to enter the kingdom of God. The disciples were dismayed. If the rich, in their privileged position, cannot be saved, who can? This is exactly the point Jesus is making. No one can save themself.

Peter and the other disciples had left their homes, jobs, and families. They had nothing else to depend upon except Jesus. What would their fate be? Jesus answered with the wild calculus of the kingdom. Anytime someone leaves someone or something dear for the sake of the kingdom, they will receive a multiplied number of the same in return. Through the family of believers they joined when they followed Jesus, God gave these disciples a spiritual family as they traveled. They gained brothers and sisters, houses to stay in as they walked toward Jerusalem, and spiritual children and cousins far greater in number than their own biological families. The point is this: whatever you give up for the kingdom, it's worth it. God sees your sacrifice, and he will reward you for it.

Luke 18:31-43. God was the purposeful director of the final weeks and months of Jesus's life. Jesus had clarity about his calling and willingly walked toward Jerusalem. The disciples understood none of this. They still had not grasped the call of the suffering servant. So not only did Jesus have to bear the anticipation of his agony; he had to do so alone.

The blind beggar stands in juxtaposition to the rich young ruler and the proud Pharisee like a beacon of hope. From Mark, we know his name as Bartimaeus. He was completely aware of his need and shamelessly cried to Jesus for help. He lived out exactly what Jesus encouraged in both the story of the neighbor at midnight (Luke 11:5-13) and the persistent widow (Luke 18:1-8). He called Jesus the "Son of David," a messianic designation, the same title that later angered the Pharisees when the children used it to refer to Jesus in their song upon his entry to Jerusalem. The Pharisee was proud, self-satisfied, and oblivious to his need. Bartimaeus was humble, desperate, and cried out for help. The rich young ruler went away sad. Bartimaeus jumped to respond to Jesus.

Luke 19:1-10. Surely the Holy Spirit had been working in Zacchaeus. From a worldly standpoint he had everything one could want. Though a Jew, he was the chief tax collector. It is hard to overstate the corruption involved in this occupation at the time. Over the years Zacchaeus became rich by stealing from others. The Jews hated him because of this. He was considered a traitor to his own people, an outcast, a sinner—exactly the kind of person to whom Jesus seemed to be drawn.

Jesus looked at Zacchaeus, called him by name, and invited himself to be Zacchaeus's houseguest. This, of course, angered everyone around him. They still didn't understand the kind of people with whom Jesus regularly socialized. But something was happening in Zacchaeus's heart: faith was being born. He responded to Jesus in true repentance, changing his practice, making amends. He was the camel who went through the eye of the needle, the rich man who was saved—impossible until Jesus made it possible. He was one of the lost whom Jesus had come to seek and save. Because of his faith, he, too, was considered a son of Abraham.

Luke 19:11–27. Jesus had tried multiple times using plain words to explain to the disciples what would happen in Jerusalem—that he would be tortured and killed. Still, they continued to have some notion of Jesus leading a military takeover or a political uprising. As they approached the city, Jesus told this parable to prepare them for the fact that he was not about to take over and reign as an earthly king but instead would leave them in charge of the church.

In the parable, the nobleman entrusted his servants with his money, expecting them to grow his investment. The servants hated the nobleman and did not want the man to reign over them, just as the Jews repeatedly rejected Jesus and his ministry. The man returned, and he called the servants to account. The reward for the first two servants for stewarding the money well was more responsibility. But the last man hid the money, not understanding that it had been given to him in order to make good use of it for the king. The Lord stands before us now and issues the same charge; we must use the spiritual gifts, abilities, money, power, and positions we have now on earth for the sake of the growth of the kingdom. Our reward in the new heavens and new earth will be even greater authority and responsibility entrusted to us by the king himself. Those who refuse to submit their resources to Jesus as they wait for his return will eventually be judged by him.

Luke 19:28–40. Jesus's disciples had been waiting for this moment. They had watched him work miracles, listened to him teach, been privy to his teaching on prayer and his surprising intimacy with God, his Father. They were convinced he was the

Messiah, the one they had been waiting for. And now they believed the time had finally come for everyone else to see who he was, to celebrate, and to praise God as Jesus came to set up his kingdom in Jerusalem. And so they shouted, sang, and yelled with joy. This must have seemed like a victory parade as they loudly approached the city.

The Pharisees took it in—Jesus entering the city on a donkey that had never been ridden before, the disciples' garments spread on the ground, the crowd's praises to a king—and for once they didn't miss the significance. This was nothing less than the messianic entrance to the city of Zion foretold in the Scriptures. No wonder they told the crowd to be quiet. But Jesus let them sing and shout. Essentially, he said, "The stones along this path know who I am though you do not. And if the people here do not worship me, they will."

Luke 19:41-44. The contrast between what was happening in the crowd and the emotion that Jesus exhibited is astonishing. While there were shouts of joy, triumph, and victory from the disciples around him, Jesus burst into tears, sobbing. As he saw the great city of Jerusalem, he wept because of its coming destruction. There would be no peace in Jerusalem. The Prince of Peace had visited and had been rejected by the religious leaders. Because of this, judgment was coming. This elicited great waves of compassion and disappointment from Jesus.

Luke 19:45–48. It was not the trading of coins or the selling of animals that angered Jesus; it was where they were doing it. They had stationed themselves in the only area of the temple where Gentiles were allowed to pray. Isaiah 56:7 named the temple as a place where all nations could pray and sacrifice to God. But these merchants robbed any non-Jews of their prescribed place to communicate with and worship their God. This elicited hot anger from Jesus.

Jesus had come to the city of peace to establish his kingdom, but not the kingdom that his disciples or anyone else expected. The servant king had purposely traveled to Jerusalem to be rejected and killed by those who should have recognized and worshiped him. Even now Jesus invites us to trust him and to enter into peace with God.

In the kingdom of Jesus, lepers were healed and it was the Samaritan that turned to thank him. He promised a return that was unexpected but better than anything that could be given up in this life. Jesus came that there might be a way to God. He came to die, to rise, to reign. He came to love us, the servant king.

Reflection Questions

5. Jesus sent the lepers to the priest as if they were already clean, and they were cleansed on the way. Where is God asking you to trust him and his words before you see evidence of his work? What about that is hard for you?

6. Jesus used an unrighteous judge and a persistent widow to teach his followers about how to pray, specifically to pray for justice. Is this how you pray? What areas of justice is the Lord calling you to intercede for?

7. The rich young ruler trusted in his wealth. What do you trust in as much as or more than you trust in the Lord? What would repentance and change look like in this area?

8. As you reflect on the agony Jesus knew he was going to face completely alone on the cross, what is your response?

9. Think of the beautiful moment and all the Scripture fulfilled as Jesus rode into Jerusalem on a donkey. What do you find most glorious about this moment?

Study 8: The Weeping King (Luke 17–19)

Focus verse: *Being asked by the Pharisees when the kingdom of God would come, he answered them, "The kingdom of God is not coming in ways that can be observed, nor will they say, 'Look, here it is!' or 'There!' for behold, the kingdom of God is in the midst of you."*
Luke 17:20-21

Reflections, curiosities, frustrations:

Study 9

The Sovereign King

Read Luke 20–22

Observation Questions

1. What happens in the parable of the wicked tenants (Luke 20:9-18)?

2. In Luke 21:5-19, what are some things Jesus said would happen before the end comes? List some ways he told his listeners to respond.

3. In Luke 22:24-30, what does Jesus tell his disciples when they dispute who is the greatest? What does he tell Simon Peter in Luke 22:31-34?

4. In Luke 22:39-46, what is Jesus's conversation with his Father? What did he say to his disciples?

Luke 20:1-8. Those who held power among the Jewish people had made their decision: Jesus must die. Now they had to figure out a plan. First, representatives from the Sanhedrin, the highest court of justice for the Jews, questioned Jesus about his teaching. They were attempting to get him to commit what they would have considered blasphemy by admitting that his authority was from God.

But Jesus was secure in his identity as God's Son and his calling to die in Jerusalem. He knew they were trying to trap him, so he raised the stakes by asking about John. The leaders were stuck. If they said that John's baptism was from heaven, they admitted failure for not believing him. If they said John's baptism was from men, they feared stoning by the people, which was the punishment for calling a true prophet of God a false prophet. Jesus had outwitted them. Their only option was to plead ignorance.

Luke 20:9-18. Jesus used a parable with images from Isaiah 5:1–7 to explain the relationship between God and Israel. The vineyard was a place of blessing that belonged to God, who lent it out to Israel to be cared for and tended. God sent his servants, the prophets, as messengers to Israel. Each of them were mistreated. While God, like the owner, had every right to punish the tenants after the very first servant was poorly treated, he was patient. In his compassion, God sent more messengers and eventually sent his Son, whom they would kill. His death would mean that the blessed vineyard would be handed over to others.

The Jewish leaders understood that Jesus was talking about them, and therefore about the blessing being taken from Israel and given to Gentiles—those outside Israel. This was unthinkable to them, and they said, "Surely not!" Jesus then quoted Psalm 118:22, explaining that the one rejected by the Jews would become the most important one in the church—God's new Israel. The cornerstone held together two intersecting walls and guaranteed their stability. Jesus was the cornerstone, laid by God.

Luke 20:19-26. The scribes and chief priests tried another tactic. Instead of trying to trap Jesus themselves, they hired spies who pretended to be righteous and interested in Jesus's teaching. The spies thought they could catch Jesus as he chose one loyalty or the other—the government or God. But just as he had done with the conversation about John's baptism, he turned the tables on them. Jesus's reply explained that we are citizens of earth and heaven at the same time. Honoring an earthly government's authority is actually part of what it means to honor and submit to God.

Luke 20:27-40. The Sadducees' question was engineered to show the foolishness of the idea of resurrection. With the ridiculous example of the woman with seven husbands, the Sadducees thought they had trapped Jesus. Not so. First, he corrected their mistaken assumptions about life after death, explaining that the next life will be different in its relational realities. Second, Jesus knew that the Sadducees only believed in the Torah (the first five books of the Bible as given to Moses), and he argued from it. He explained that there must be a resurrection. In Exodus 3:6, God said to Moses out of the burning bush, "I am the God of your father, the God of Abraham, the God of Isaac, and the God of Jacob." All three of those men were dead when God spoke to Moses. Therefore, if he was still their God, resurrection must be a reality.

Luke 20:45-47. The scribes were not allowed to charge money for their teaching, but they often received gifts. Some were thought to have talked widows into giving larger gifts than they could afford, and others may have charged commissions for handling the legal affairs of widows. These men would be judged for their actions.

Luke 21:1-4. The poor widow gave two of the smallest coins in circulation at the time, all she had to buy the basic necessities for life. The rich had gone before her, contributing who-knows-how-much out of their wealth. But Jesus didn't measure the gifts by the amount given; he measured by the amount kept. By this measure, the widow had given, in Jesus's words, "more than all of them."

Here again we see the upside-down kingdom of Jesus. This widow, surely the poorest and therefore last in her culture, had become the first, as Jesus commended her. The rich, who were considered first in terms of money, influence, and power, who lived in arrogance and sparred with Jesus, were all outwitted by him, condemned by him. They had become last.

Luke 21:5-19. Even as some people with Jesus were admiring the beauty of the temple structure, he explained that it would be destroyed. They wanted to know when this would happen and what events would immediately precede it. Jesus did not answer with one specific event to look for but warned his disciples of the chaos that was coming.

When he said, "But not a hair of your head will perish," Jesus was not promising the physical safety of his disciples; rather he was saying that absolute, permanent destruction was not possible for the believer. There is something much worse than physical death—eternal condemnation. As believers, we are secure in our connection to Christ. Because he rose, we will as well. Death cannot prevent our resurrection.

Luke 21:20-24. Jesus continued to describe the events that would come to pass in the destruction of Jerusalem. Usually when war came in this era, rural people would come into the cities surrounded by walls for protection. Jesus instructed his followers to do the opposite and run to the mountains. He was clear that this was the judgment of God. Many would be killed, others would be taken captive, and the city would be demolished. Historians tell us that this is exactly what happened in the siege of Jerusalem in 70 AD.

Luke 21:25-28. Most scholars agree that in verse 25 Jesus moves from describing the events preceding the fall of Jerusalem to a description of the events preceding the last judgment, the end of the world as we know it, his return. Remember that these are actual instructions given by Jesus to a specific group of people in the future. Those people may be us, they may be our great grandchildren, or they may be a generation hundreds or thousands of years from now. But Jesus encourages them to "raise their heads" when these signs come, for their total liberation is about to take place.

Luke 21:29–33. The disciples had asked for a sign. Here Jesus replied with a parable: Just as the fig tree gives signs of summer nearing, so these things are signs of the kingdom of God nearing. "Generation" probably refers here to humans in general and the way that they consistently reject Jesus and his message. Just as there were people rejecting Jesus and the gospel while he walked on the earth, so there will be when he comes a second time. Still, his promise to return is more trustworthy than creation itself.

Luke 21:34–38. Jesus ended his instructions about the siege of Jerusalem and his own return with a warning: We must watch ourselves, literally "pay attention." Jesus is telling us to be careful not to misuse our energy or to numb ourselves as we wait for him to return.

Luke 22:1–6. Remember that when Satan left Jesus in the wilderness, he "left him until an opportune time" (Luke 4:13). That opportune time had come. Satan entered Judas and apparently prompted him to offer himself as a covert link from the Sanhedrin to Jesus. Of course, the chief priests and temple officers were delighted. So Judas began the quiet search for an opportunity to hand Jesus over.

Luke 22:7–13. The Jews celebrated the Passover meal in a very specific way, and preparation for such a meal would have taken time and effort. Apparently Jesus had arranged a place to eat the meal with his disciples days earlier. Notice all of the signs and code Jesus used. All of this was planned and timed by the Lord. Jesus was in control, even in this moment.

Luke 22:14–20. As Jesus had done over and over, he named what was coming: his suffering. From this passage we understand that the bread of the meal symbolized Jesus's body. The apostles would have understood that Israel had been in a covenant relationship with God. They would have had a clear understanding of the fact that the blood of animals was involved in the covenant made between God and their great patriarch Abraham. Now, Jesus was establishing that his blood was involved in the new covenant he was implementing. His blood would be poured out for them just as the blood of animals had been in the old covenant. As they had eaten the lamb of the first exodus meal, so Jesus was the new lamb of the new exodus meal.

Luke 22:21-30. The ESV's "as it has been determined" and the NIV's "as it has been decreed" represent a voice known as the divine passive. Though his name is not mentioned, God is the subject of this sentence. He is the one who determined and decreed that these things would take place. And yet, the human who acts to bring them to pass is still held responsible. "Woe to that man!" says Jesus. He does not resolve for us the tension of human responsibility and divine sovereignty.

Luke 22:31-38. The "you" in verse 31 is plural, meaning that Satan asked permission from God to sift all of the disciples, separating the good from the bad, attempting perhaps to separate them from God by intense testing. The "you" in verse 32 is singular, indicating that Jesus was speaking to Peter specifically. Jesus knew that he would fail, knew he would return, and expected him to encourage and strengthen all the others when he did. The failure of Peter, the spokesperson for the disciples, the one on whom the church was built, was expected, accounted for, and used by the king himself.

Luke 22:39-46. Jesus knew that he would die physically when turned over to the Roman authorities; that would actually be the lesser of the evils he faced. The greater would be facing the wrath of his Father. Jesus, the Second Person of the Trinity, had only ever known perfect communion and relationship with his Father. But in his death, he would face the "cup," the absolute hate, fury, displeasure, and punishment of a holy God toward all of the sin ever committed in the past or future.

We can learn much from this short passage about how to walk through our own suffering and trials. Jesus did not "stay strong" or "keep a stiff upper lip," ignoring his emotions or pretending not to struggle when he was filled with anxiety. He was honest with God, vulnerable, asking for help. See his humanity and his wrestling with God's will. He begged God three times to change his mind. But as he grappled with what God was calling him to do, he submitted himself, consenting on his knees to be the object of all of God's wrath.

Luke 22:47–53. Jesus named the strangeness of the Jewish leaders coming to arrest him under cover of darkness, though he had regularly been in the temple for all to see. Unlike most revolutionaries who hid in the mountains, Jesus had not hidden from anyone. It was the actions of the Sanhedrin that were shifty.

Luke 22:54–62. Perhaps Jesus was being led from one part of the house to the other and happened to be in Peter's line of sight at that moment. Maybe he was in a part of the house visible to the courtyard. However it happened, at the moment of Peter's third denial, the Lord was able to look directly at Peter. While we may expect that this was a look of disappointment, anger, or "I told you so," Luke's word choice tells us otherwise. This Greek word, *emblepō*, refers to a "look of interest, love, or concern." This was a look of compassion from Jesus in the moment of his disciple's epic failure. Jesus didn't rub his nose in it, punish him, or even become angry. He had compassion on Peter. Does he not take the same posture toward us in the midst of our own failures to love him?

Luke 22:63–71. While none of the Gospels give us every detail of Jesus's sham trial, piecing them together tells us that there were basically two stages: trial by the Jews and then trial by the Romans. The Jewish leaders wanted to know if Jesus was claiming to be the Christ awaited by their people. He answered them, yes, and no: Yes, I am the Christ, but not the one you were expecting. The Jews didn't care that Jesus's kingdom was a totally different kingdom than what they were asking about. For them, his own words condemned him.

Again, consider Jesus's power and ability to extract himself from this situation. Up to this point he had resisted the pointed temptations of Satan in the desert. He had healed thousands from various diseases and released hundreds from Satan's grip of demon possession. He had allowed some of his glory to show forth on the mountain in front of Peter, James, and John. He had bested the Pharisees, scribes, and others over and over in their arguments, slipped through their word traps, and surpassed their ability to debate to the point that "they no longer dared to ask him any question" (Luke 20:40). Obviously, it was entirely within his power and ability to stop this chain of events. And yet he did not. Over and over he allowed things to happen that he could have stopped. It was no accident that he was betrayed, handed over, and found guilty. He had come to Jerusalem to die for the sins of the world, and this unjust, sneaky mess of events was how he would do it.

Dear one, see even in this moment his absolute sovereignty and vulnerability. That he would submit himself to such squabbling and prideful men in order to accomplish his goal of your redemption. This is how the servant king would win your salvation. This is how he would drink the cup of God's wrath, that you might never taste it. He came to die, to rise, to reign. He came to love us, the servant king.

Reflection Questions

5. Jesus's response to the widow's meager gift as being the most shows that Jesus measures intentions of the heart over the size of the gift. As you reflect on giving out of your poverty instead of out of your abundance, what thought comes to mind?

6. Jesus calls us to be watchful as we wait for his return. What are some things that keep you from watchfulness in your life? How do these things weigh your heart down?

7. As Jesus gets even closer to his death, he goes to great lengths to serve and teach his disciples. How does viewing this up close deepen your understanding of him?

8. When Peter betrayed Jesus, as Jesus said he would, Jesus looked at Peter not with "I told you so" but with compassion. Are you surprised by this? Why or why not?

9. Jesus, being fully God, could have stopped this whole chain of events and not taken the cup of God's wrath on the cross for you. He did this because you are utterly incapable of doing it. What is your reflection on how intentionally he did this?

Focus verse: *And then they will see the Son of Man coming in a cloud with power and great glory. Now when these things begin to take place, straighten up and raise your heads, because your redemption is drawing near.*
Luke 21:27–28

Reflections, curiosities, frustrations:

Study 10

The Ascended King

Read Luke 23–24

Observation Questions

1. In Luke 23:1-5, what happened in the interaction between Pilate and Jesus?

2. Write down the details of the conversation Jesus had with the two convicted criminals who were crucified with him (Luke 23:32-43).

3. In Luke 24:1-12, who went to the tomb? Who was there? What happened when they told the apostles?

4. In Luke 24:36-43, what did Jesus show his disciples to help them believe it was him? What did he ask for from them?

Luke 23:1-5. The Jewish leaders had made their decision; Jesus was guilty. The Sanhedrin had no power to hand out the death penalty; only Rome could do that. But what did Rome care if some Jew offended the other Jews' religious beliefs? The Jewish leaders had to make accusations Rome would care about. The Jewish leaders' first charge, that Jesus was undermining the power and authority of Rome, could have been said about many and was ignored. The second, that Jesus opposed the paying of taxes to Caesar, was clearly false (see Luke 20:20–26). But a claim to be king was political in nature, and Pilate could not ignore such an allegation. As he had the night before, Jesus answered yes but did not explain the true character of his kingdom. Yes, he was king of the Jews, but not king in the way Pilate would have understood kingship. Pilate recognized the charges brought against Jesus were absurd. Jesus was innocent of all crimes.

Luke 23:6–16. The Sanhedrin's mention of Galilee offered Pilate the opportunity to shift legal responsibility to Herod, the local Roman authority in charge of that province. Herod was also in Jerusalem for the Passover, and he was excited to see some sort of show from Jesus. However, when Herod questioned Jesus, he received only silence. While Jesus was always ready to engage with true seekers, he would not perform circus tricks for this official who had no real spiritual curiosity. Disappointed, Herod joined his soldiers in mocking Jesus. At this point, two Roman officials had examined Jesus and found him innocent.

Luke 23:18–25. Again we see the intertwining of God's sovereignty and human responsibility. Pilate was and is responsible for this action. He was given authority at the time and place of Jesus's trial, and he should have acted on behalf of the innocent man. At the same time, just as God used Judas's betrayal in order to work his plan of redemption, so he worked through Pilate. He used this particular rivalry of power between the Jews and Rome, the anger, pride, and jealousy of the Jewish leadership, and the relationships between Herod and Pilate to walk his own Son to execution. He can employ any political dynamic, any relationship, any cultural norm, any person or anything anywhere for his own purpose and desire. If he utilized such a sham trial for the process of his Son's death and the ultimate redemption of the world, how much more can he use our seemingly hopeless circumstances to accomplish his glory and our good?

The guilty man was released, while the innocent man was sentenced to death. It is worth pausing to consider that Jesus was walking to death in order to pay for the sins of Barabbas, a guilty man. Surely this is the upside-down kingdom, where the blameless king would choose to die for the guilty.

Luke 23:26–31. The terrible day had finally come. Jesus had been making his way toward Jerusalem for months in order to give himself up to the Jews, to the Romans, and to the cross. The beating that usually preceded crucifixion was so extreme that it often caused the death of the prisoner. Jesus had survived the beating but was weak enough that he could no longer carry the crossbeam that condemned persons were required to transport on their back, so the Roman guards forced a passerby into service. The fact that Simon's two sons are mentioned by name in Mark 15:21 hints that Simon may have become a follower of Jesus through this encounter. He was the first to literally take up his cross and follow the king.

Jesus told the crowd to weep not for him but for themselves. He knew that Jerusalem would be judged for what they were doing to him. While Jews considered it a terrible misfortune not to be able to have children, Jesus was telling them that the destruction of Jerusalem would bring with it suffering so terrible that barrenness at that point would be preferred. Then, in verse 31, Jesus asked a terrifying question: If I, the innocent man (the green wood), suffer like this on a cross, how will the guilty men, the Jews who rejected me (the dry wood), suffer?

Luke 23:32–34. Jesus's death among criminals fulfilled the prophecy of Isaiah 53:12, "he poured out his soul to death and was numbered with the transgressors." It is in this moment of hanging between two thieves that he asked his Father to forgive "them," probably referring both to the Jews who brought charges against him and the Romans who actually implemented the sentence.

Luke 23:35–43. The irony of the taunts from the rulers and the soldiers was that if Jesus would have saved himself, he could not have saved anyone else. Jesus's crime was that he claimed to be king, a political infraction in the eyes of Rome. Again, the irony was that not only was it true—Jesus actually was and is king—but believing and acknowledging that truth could have saved everyone watching the scene. One of the thieves mocked Jesus along with the rulers and soldiers, but the other recognized his kingship, asking Jesus to remember him. Jesus could have shamed him, rejected him, required certain words, or even scared him. But Jesus is never one to shame or reject anyone who asks for him in faith. Instead he promised him paradise.

Luke 23:44-49. The curtain that ripped was between the Holy Place and the Holy of Holies, where only the high priest was allowed to go once per year to atone for the sins of the people. With his death, Jesus eliminated any barrier between himself and his people. The curtain was no longer needed. The sin that kept Israel and all of us apart from a holy God had been paid for by the punishment of the sinless man.

Notice the different reactions of those watching Jesus. Some mocked him. Others belittled or taunted. Some mourned or felt guilty, while at least one confessed Jesus's true identity. All must respond to the life, death, and resurrection of this king. What will your response be?

Luke 23:50-56. According to Jewish law, a body could not remain hanging after sundown. Since the Sabbath was about to begin, the body was wrapped, hurriedly prepared, then placed in the tomb. When the women saw how Jesus's body was placed, they apparently deemed it inadequate and returned home to prepare spices and perfumes to use on his body when the Sabbath was over. These spices were what they would be carrying in their hands Sunday morning when they walked to his tomb.

Luke 24:1-12. It did not immediately occur to the women that Jesus had been raised from the dead. He had explained exactly what would happen to him multiple times—and even told them about his resurrection—but none of his followers had fully grasped his plan. And so God sent angels. The women's response mirrored Mary's and Zechariah's responses in Luke 1, when they both received angelic visitors. These were radiant, powerful, holy beings who suddenly appeared. It is no wonder the humans were terrified.

The angels were there to explain again what Jesus had already foretold. They reminded the women of Jesus's words. When the women heard the words again spoken by the angels, they remembered. The full import of what had happened must have settled in their minds as they ran back from the tomb to the apostles.

It is noteworthy that women were the first witnesses of the resurrection. In Jesus's day the testimony of women was unacceptable, and inadmissible in a court of law. But Luke, who repeatedly pointed out Jesus's dignifying interactions with women, did so this one last time. Just as Mary had the privilege of being the first to know of Jesus's incarnation in Luke 1, so these women were the first to learn of his resurrection. When the women reached the other disciples, ten of the apostles flat out didn't believe. Peter actually ran to the tomb to look but only left confused and bewildered. It would take more witnesses to convince the eleven that Jesus was alive.

Luke 24:13–24. Apparently Jesus walked right up alongside these two, though they were kept from recognizing him. When he asked them his question, they stopped, obviously sad. Jesus had been killed by the Romans, and the consensus among his followers was that he must not have been the Christ. Even explaining the announcement of the women and the words of the angel had not convinced them. They had believed up to the point of his suffering and death, but those things did not fit in with their understanding of the Messiah.

Luke 24:25-35. These followers of Jesus had expected the glory but not the suffering of the Messiah. They expected that the redeemer of the Jews would experience victory and authority but not that he would ever submit to pain or suffering. When he died on the cross, their hopes were dashed. Jesus corrected their understanding using the Old Testament. He showed them that the Old Testament law and all of the prophets pointed to him. He was not a new idea drummed up for the current generation. Rather, he was the hope and fulfillment of all of God's promises from the very beginning.

It was while communing with him over the meal that God opened their eyes to finally recognize Jesus. Apparently they did not even take time to finish their meal but went straight back to the city to tell the other disciples that they had seen the Lord. They had finally understood that Jesus had been resurrected. As the hours of the day went on and more and more of his followers were allowed to see and understand the reality of Jesus's resurrection, their joy and hope must have grown. He appeared to them first in pairs or small groups, but God had to open their eyes to actually see the truth, and it was with one another that they confirmed these things and grew in confidence about what they had seen.

Luke 24:36-43. Jesus's followers had been trying to put the pieces together and understand exactly what had happened when Jesus appeared among them. These disciples were still confused about what they were seeing. Was this simply the spirit of Jesus, coming to visit them from the dead? Was this someone else? The God-man who had just accomplished the defeat of death condescended to the limited minds of these disciples and showed himself to them. He offered his hands and feet as proof, allowing them to touch his body.

Still they did not believe. But this time it was because of their joy and amazement. This was too good to be true. It was beyond their ability to comprehend at the moment. Of course,

Jesus knew this. He understood their limits, their fear, their confusion. And so he gave them tactile, sensory ways to see his humanity. He ate in front of them. This is Jesus's posture toward doubting, confused disciples. He extends himself to them in ways they can grasp. He patiently shows himself to those who seek him, even in the midst of disbelief.

Luke 24:44–49. Jesus was no longer "with them" as he had been while on earth. Now his presence was different, the exception rather than the norm. He repeated the words he had said while he lived on earth: "Everything written about me in the Law of Moses and the Prophets and the Psalms must be fulfilled." Again Jesus explained that all of the Scriptures, the types, the stories, and the foreshadowings were pointing to him. He had made statements like these before, and indeed quoted the Old Testament in regard to himself throughout his ministry. But until he opened their minds to understand, they could not.

Jesus outlined the storyline of the Christ as taught in the Old Testament—he would suffer; he would rise from the dead on the third day; and in his name, repentance and forgiveness of sins would be proclaimed to all nations. From the beginning, even in the covenant with Abraham, God had intended his promise to be extended outside the nation of Israel.

Jesus tells them they were to be the witnesses. How would a frightened, doubting group of people ever become the means by which all nations might know about repentance and forgiveness of sins? Only by Jesus sending the promise of his Father, the Holy Spirit. The disciples were to remain in the city until they were "clothed" with his power. This, too, was prophesied long before the incarnation of Jesus (see Joel 2:28). It had always been God's plan to give the Holy Spirit to his disciples in the last days in order that they might carry out the mission of announcing the kingdom to all nations. Only God could equip his children for such a task.

Luke 24:50–53. It is easy to think that the story is basically over. We can sometimes skip over the ascension like the notes at the back of the book—necessary but expected, more of a placeholder than a life-changer. But the ascension is not an afterthought or a way to wrap up the story. The ascension is the coronation of the king, the finishing of his work, the beginning of his heavenly reign and of his giving of gifts to the church. The true triumphal entry happened when the King of Kings, having accomplished his work on earth, returned to heaven as the exalted king.

The servant king was born into poverty, lived a perfect life, drank the cup of wrath for us, defeated death, and ascended to the throne, bringing us with him. May we join our voices with those of the disciples at the end of Luke and praise our God for his perfect work of redemption. He came to die, to rise, to reign. He came to love us, the servant king.

Reflection Questions

5. Justice was not given to Jesus. Even though he was innocent and proven so by Herod and Pilate, he was still sent to be crucified. God worked the most important moment in human history through injustice. What are your thoughts as you reflect on this?

6. As the women following Jesus were mourning him, he told them that he was mourning for what was to come for them despite the agony he was about to face. What does this demonstrate to us about how Jesus loves and serves us?

7. Even though Jesus had told the apostles several times that he would die and rise again, they were slow to believe when it happened. What words of Jesus are you slow to believe?

8. Despite all the evidence before Jesus's followers' eyes, the resurrection was still hard to grasp. Jesus met them in that by doing such things as eating in front of them and showing them his scars. What does this show us about God meeting us wholistically in our unbelief?

9. Christ ascended to glory, his royal kingly coronation, representing us, the redeemed, there. Write a prayer to Jesus in thankfulness for this.

Focus verse: *Then he opened their minds to understand the Scriptures, and said to them, "Thus it is written, that the Christ should suffer and on the third day rise from the dead, and that repentance for the forgiveness of sins should be proclaimed in his name to all nations, beginning from Jerusalem. You are witnesses of these things. And behold, I am sending the promise of my Father upon you. But stay in the city until you are clothed with power from on high."*
Luke 24:45–49

Reflections, curiosities, frustrations:

Acknowledgments

Christine: Michael, you said to do this years ago. Sorry it took so long. Thanks for your patience. Marcia, you continue to broaden your heavenly investment portfolio. It will bring you a good return. Jacob, I kind of can't believe you're still willing to stay on this crazy ride with us. Thank you for being so patient and steady. Renae, I still can't believe you managed to do this. God gave you just what we need. Jen, here is another book produced in part by your encouragement and prayers. Hope, I think it goes without saying, but this time I just have to say it: you're one of my greatest pleasures. So thankful to do this with you.

Hope: Thank you to the host of people who are always cheering and encouraging this work: Ray, Mom and Dad, the Sisters, our advisory committee, and so many other friends along the way. This book was born out of wanting to reach our sisters that are in hard to reach places spiritually due to their story, their language, or their context. This book is for you and may you meet Christ through it. Renae, you are a master sculptor, and this book is proof! So grateful for you. Jen your prayers have brought many things to life—love having you along in this. Chris, seriously the most lavish of gifts—all of it.

A Note on Sources

I have drawn from a wealth of other people's hard work in my study of Luke. I am first indebted to Dr. Dan Doriani, who taught Gospels at Covenant Seminary with such excellence and who also directed me to specific commentators to be trusted in their treatment of the text. I have relied on biblehub.com for their excellent Greek interlinear verses and their commentators, specifically Clarke and Ellicott. I have used monergism.com multiple times to access sermons, especially those of Sinclair Ferguson and Alistair Begg. I have also consulted Bruce J. Malina's *The New Testament World, Insights from Cultural Anthropology* (Westminster/John Knox Press, 1993). What a wonderful resource for understanding the world in which Jesus lived.

Other At His Feet Studies

We pray that you will continue to sit at the feet of Jesus, studying his Word. To help you with this, we have also written Bible studies for women on these books of the Bible:

Romans (28 studies)

1 Samuel (16 studies)

Philippians (12 studies)

Psalms (13 studies)

Luke: Part 1 (13 studies)

Luke: Part 2 (14 studies)

Luke: Part 3 (12 studies)

Galatians (8 studies)